Math Connections to the Real World

Author: LINDA ARMSTRONG
Editor: MARY DIETERICH
Proofreaders: APRIL ALBERT and MARGARET BROWN

COPYRIGHT © 2016 Mark Twain Media, Inc.

ISBN 978-1-62223-597-1

Printing No. CD-404252

Mark Twain Media, Inc., Publishers
Distributed by Carson-Dellosa Publishing LLC

Visit us at www.carsondellosa.com

Table of Contents

Table of Contents (cont.)

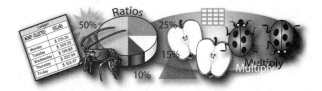

Introduction to the Teacher

To solve word problems effectively, students must determine what is being asked, locate relevant information, and decide which operation to perform before they carry out any calculations. The same comprehension skills that support students in literature, history, and science are essential for solving word problems in math. While making students more aware of the practical applications of mathematics in their daily lives, guided practice with word and logic problems can help them become more focused readers.

The question is the heart of any word problem. It is easy, but ultimately frustrating, to waste precious time and energy chasing down the answer to a question that was not asked. After skimming the material, students should imagine that they are detectives and make sure they understand what their "client" wants to know. Encourage them to ferret out question words and phrases.

For example, the question might ask "Which boy is the fastest?" Although students would use an operation involving numbers to solve the problem, the answer to the question would be a name.

Sample question words and phrases:

How many	*How far*	*How long*	*Which*	*What time*
What	*Who*	*Where*	*Why*	

With the question in mind, students need to determine which information is relevant. In most textbook problems, all of the information offered will be used in some way, but in the real world, this is not true. As a result, test-makers often include extra facts in their paragraphs. Students should read carefully and select only the information that will help them find the answer.

Once they have isolated relevant facts, problem-solvers must select the proper operation. Certain words are often clues.

Sample clue words and phrases:	Operation Required:
• *in all*	addition or multiplication
• *all together*	addition or multiplication
• *how many more than*	subtraction
• *how much larger than*	subtraction
• *to the nearest*	rounding off or estimation
• *about*	estimation
• *of*	multiplication of fractions
• *how many ____ are there in*	division

Math Connections to the Real World is designed to increase students' ability to use math effectively in their schoolwork as well as in their everyday lives. As students develop their knowledge and understanding of grammatical usage, punctuation, and capitalization, their ability to comprehend the word problems, effectively solve them, and then communicate the answers verbally and in writing will also improve.

Encourage students to use dictionaries, thesauruses, and other reference sources when working on activities. After all, a student can't use a word correctly if he or she does not know its meaning.

Introduction to the Teacher (cont.)

Topics Covered

The activities in this book focus on skills that enable students to:

- use mathematical operations in everyday situations;
- determine questions, find relevant facts, and select appropriate operations;
- estimate results and check their own calculations;
- unleash the real-world power of place value;
- gather and interpret data;
- create drawings, diagrams, and other models to solve problems;
- perform basic, practical operations with fractions and decimals;
- reduce fractions to their lowest terms and convert them to their decimal equivalents;
- understand the importance of equivalence when working with proportions, ratios, fractions, and basic equations;
- perform operations with U.S. standard and/or metric measures of length, weight, and volume;
- perform basic operations with money;
- work with elapsed time, speed, distance, and differences between time zones;
- use ordered pairs of integers to locate points on a map, graph, or axis;
- read and/or generate bar graphs, pie graphs, line graphs, and pictographs;
- use information presented in Venn diagrams to solve problems;
- recognize the properties of lines, shapes, and forms;
- find the perimeters of polygons;
- use formulae to find the perimeter of a circle and the area of a triangle;
- solve problems requiring more than one operation; and
- solve logic problems.

Suggestions for Use

Each activity page is divided into two reproducible sections that can be cut apart and used separately. Activities could be used in class as warm-ups or for review either with a group or individually. Transparencies of the activities can encourage student participation as they follow along when a new concept is introduced. Extra copies can be kept in your learning center for review and additional practice, or copies can be distributed as homework assignments.

Organization

Activities are arranged by skill level and topic and are progressively more difficult. Later activities build on knowledge covered earlier in the book.

Since reading comprehension and the use of reasoning are skills being assessed in most state and national standardized tests, this book will help students master those skills.

The table of contents identifies the skills that students use to complete each activity. The skills are also listed on each activity just below the title. An answer key is provided at the end of the book. A matrix of skills addressed by each activity, based on NCTM standards, is also included.

NCTM Standards Matrix for Grades 5–8

Problem Solving

- Build new mathematical knowledge through problem solving—**Level 1:** pg. 1–18; **Level 2:** pg. 19–34; **Level 3:** pg. 35–52

- Solve problems that arise in mathematics and in other contexts—**Level 1:** pg. 1–18; **Level 2:** pg. 19–34; **Level 3:** pg. 35–52

- Apply and adapt a variety of appropriate strategies to solve problems—**Level 1:** pg. 1–18; **Level 2:** pg. 19–34; **Level 3:** pg. 35–52

- Monitor and reflect on the process of mathematical problem solving—**Level 1:** pg. 1, 4, 6, 8, 9, 18; **Level 2:** pg. 19, 20, 23, 25, 26, 28–34; **Level 3:** pg. 35–37, 43–45, 47, 50, 52

Reasoning and Proof

- Recognize reasoning and proof as fundamental aspects of mathematics—**Level 1:** pg. 1, 5–7, 9, 10, 13–18; **Level 2:** pg. 18, 20, 22, 23, 26, 27, 29, 31–33; **Level 3:** pg. 35, 36, 43–45, 47, 48, 52

- Make and investigate mathematical conjectures—**Level 1:** pg. 5–7, 9, 10, 13–18; **Level 2:** pg. 18, 22–27, 29, 31–33; **Level 3:** pg. 35, 36, 43–45, 48, 50, 52

- Develop and evaluate mathematical arguments and proofs—**Level 1:** 5–7, 9, 10, 13–17; **Level 2:** pg. 20, 22, 23, 26, 27, 29, 31–33; **Level 3:** 35, 36, 43

- Select and use various types of reasoning and methods of proof—**Level 1:** pg. 1, 5–7, 9, 10, 13–17; **Level 2:** pg. 10, 22, 23, 26, 27, 29, 31–33; **Level 3:** pg. 35, 36, 43–45, 48, 50, 52

Communication

- Organize and consolidate mathematical thinking through communication—**Level 1:** pg. 1, 4, 5, 10–17; **Level 2:** pg. 19–21, 24–31; **Level 3:** pg. 35–52

- Communicate mathematical thinking coherently and clearly to peers, teachers, and others—**Level 1:** pg. 1, 4, 10–17; **Level 2:** pg. 19–22, 24, 25, 31; **Level 3:** pg. 35–52

- Analyze and evaluate the mathematical thinking and strategies of others—**Level 1:** pg. 1, 5, 10–18; **Level 2:** pg. 19–21, 25, 26, 29; **Level 3:** pg. 35, 36, 43, 47

- Use the language of mathematics to express mathematical ideas precisely—**Level 1:** pg. 1, 4, 5, 10, 12–18; **Level 2:** pg. 19–22, 24–31; **Level 3:** pg. 35–52

Connections

- Recognize and use connections among mathematical ideas—**Level 1:** pg. 4–6, 9, 15, 18; **Level 2:** pg. 26–34; **Level 3:** pg. 34, 36–41, 43, 45, 48–50, 52

- Understand how mathematical ideas interconnect and build on one another to produce a coherent whole—**Level 1:** pg. 4–6, 9, 10, 15, 17, 18; **Level 2:** pg. 18–20, 22, 26–34; **Level 3:** pg. 34, 36–41, 43, 45, 48–50, 52

- Recognize and apply mathematics in contexts outside of mathematics—**Level 1:** pg. 1–18; **Level 2:** pg. 19–34; **Level 3:** pg. 35–52

Representation

- Create and use representations to organize, record, and communicate mathematical ideas—**Level 1:** pg. 2, 4–6, 10–15, 17; **Level 2:** pg. 21, 22, 24, 25, 27–28, 30–32, 34; **Level 3:** pg. 34, 35, 37, 39, 41–43, 45, 47–50, 52

- Use representation to model and interpret physical, social, and mathematical phenomena—**Level 2:** pg. 24, 32; **Level 3:** pg. 34, 35, 37, 39, 41–43, 45–50, 52

Marine Biology

Find Facts, Locate Questions, and Select Processes

Name: _____

Date: _____

To solve a word problem, first find the facts and decide what is being asked. Read the paragraph, and answer the questions.

> During a deep-sea dive, marine biologists discover four lines of spiny lobsters traveling across the sea floor. There are 62 lobsters in one line, 60 lobsters in another line, 56 lobsters in the third line, and 59 lobsters in the last line.

1. What number facts are given? _____

2. What is being counted? _____

3. Write a question that asks for a total amount, and then add to answer it. _____

   _____

4. Write a question that asks for a difference, and then subtract to answer it. _____

   _____

Organic Gardening

Place Value

Name: _____

Date: _____

Use place value to answer the questions.

> Mary likes to garden. She arranges her plants so they are easier to weed by hand. She puts one plant in the first row, two plants in the second row, and so on. She has a total of 17 rows in her garden. Answer the following questions about Mary's garden.

1. Mary grew two pumpkin plants. In which row were the pumpkins? _____

2. Peppers were in row 12. How many pepper plants did Mary have? _____

3. Mary loves fresh corn most of all. What is the biggest number of corn plants she could grow? _____

4. Watermelons were in row 5. How many watermelon plants did Mary need to buy? _____

5. Mary grew two kinds of tomato plants: paste tomatoes in row 7, and beefsteak tomatoes in row 8. Which kind of tomato did she plant more of? _____

Recycling Drive

Addition: Three Digits, No Regrouping

Read about the school's aluminum can drive, and then answer the questions.

Leo collected 730 aluminum cans during his club's recycling drive. Jeremy collected 265. Gerardo brought in 620. Jordan gathered 532, and Miguel turned in 614.

1. How many cans did Leo and Jeremy collect in all? _____

2. How many cans did Gerardo and Jordan turn in? _____

3. How many cans did Leo and Miguel turn in? _____

4. How many cans did Jeremy and Gerardo collect? _____

5. Which pair collected 797 cans? _____

Arachnid Research

**Addition: Two and Three Numbers, Three Digits
With Regrouping**

Check Dr. Martin's chart and answer the questions. You will need to regroup.

Dr. Martin was studying spider families. He caught four mother spiders and counted the baby spiders they were carrying on their backs.

1. How many baby spiders were spider moms A, B, and C

    carrying? _____

2. How many babies were spider moms B, C, and D

    carrying? _____

3. How many babies were spider moms A, B, and D

    carrying? _____

4. How many babies were all four spider moms

    carrying? _____

Spider Moms	
Spider	**No. of Babies**
Spider A	89
Spider B	96
Spider C	77
Spider D	108

Library Returns

Subtraction: Three Digits, No Regrouping

Name: _____

Date: _____

Read the paragraph and answer the questions in order.

> The public library's computer keeps track of returns. On Saturday morning, 478 books were due. By 11:30 A.M., 200 of them had been returned. By 1:30, another 150 had been returned. When the library closed at 6:00 P.M., only 10 books were still due.

1. How many books were still due at 11:30 A.M.? _____

2. How many books were still due at 1:30 P.M.? _____

3. How many books were returned between 1:30 P.M. and 6:00 P.M.? _____

   _____

4. How many of the books that were due were returned on Saturday? _____

   _____

- -

Recycling Plastics

Subtraction With Regrouping

Name: _____

Date: _____

Check the facts. Read each question carefully before answering. You will need to regroup.

> As a recycling project, Vanessa's class collected plastic bottles. On Monday, the students collected 88 bottles. On Tuesday, they collected 192. On Wednesday, they brought in 253. On Thursday, they gathered 215, and on Friday, they collected 185.

1. On Monday, the students did not bring in very many bottles. How many more did they bring in on Tuesday than on Monday? _____

2. On Wednesday, they brought in the most bottles. How many fewer did they bring on Thursday? _____

3. They brought in 88 bottles on Monday. How many more did they bring in on Friday than on Monday? _____

4. They brought in more bottles on Thursday than they did on Friday. How many more? _____

Food Bank Inventory

Mixed Addition and Subtraction

Name: _____

Date: _____

Add or subtract? You decide. Check the facts and read each question carefully.

On December 31, Baker's Beans donated 500 cans of each type of bean to the Lamar Food Bank.

1. How many cans of garbanzo beans have been given away? _____

2. How many cans of kidney beans, chili beans, and garbanzo beans are left all together?

   _____

3. How many cans of black beans have been given away?

   _____

4. How many cans of navy beans and black beans are left?

   _____

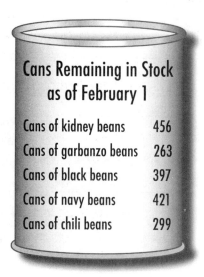

Cans Remaining in Stock as of February 1

Cans of kidney beans	456
Cans of garbanzo beans	263
Cans of black beans	397
Cans of navy beans	421
Cans of chili beans	299

Farmers Market

Mixed Addition and Subtraction

Name: _____

Date: _____

Find the clue words that tell you whether to add or subtract. Underline them, and then answer the questions.

1. How many more tomatoes than zucchinis were sold? _____

2. How many onions, tomatoes, and bunches of cilantro were sold in all? _____

3. How many potatoes and tomatoes were sold in all? _____

4. How many more bunches of cilantro than onions were sold? _____

Weekend Farm Stand Sales

potatoes	107
tomatoes	292
zucchini	163
onions	67
bunches of cilantro	276

Demographics

Round Off to Tens and Hundreds

Rounding can help you estimate answers quickly. If the number in the ones place is 5 or more, round the number in the tens place up. If the number in the tens place is 5 or more, round the number in the hundreds place up. ***Example:*** 253 would be rounded to 300, and 243 would be rounded to 200.

1. A marketer mailed out magazine subscription offers to about 8,400 people in Hesterville. According to the data table, were the offers for *Sports' Day*, *Lady's Life*, *Active Girl*, or *Today's Boy*? _____

2. The recreation center sent fliers to about 8,220 people. Did the fliers advertise a women's retreat or a men's golf tournament? _____

3. The parents of about 680 children buy clothing in local stores. Do they shop for them in the boys' department or the girls' department? _____

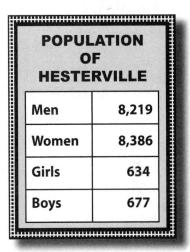

POPULATION OF HESTERVILLE

Men	8,219
Women	8,386
Girls	634
Boys	677

Waterfalls

Estimating

Round off and add to answer these questions about record-breaking waterfalls.

1. Which two falls, together, would be about 6,000 feet tall? _____ _____

2. Which two falls, together, would be about 5,300 feet tall? _____ _____

3. Which falls is about 300 feet taller than Monge Falls? _____

4. Would the height of the three falls, together, be closer to 8,000 feet or 9,000 feet? _____

Highest Waterfalls in the World

Waterfall	Height in feet
Angel Falls in Venezuela	3,212
Tugela Falls in South Africa	2,800
Monge Falls in Norway	2,540

Fruit Harvest

Multiplication: One Digit Times Two Digits

Name: _____

Date: _____

Business people use multiplication every day. Check the information, and then answer the questions.

> Mr. Dustin, a local farmer, is ready for the weekly produce market. His truck is loaded with fruit.

1. How many pears are in the truck? _____

2. Mrs. Carter is planning to make jam. She will buy all of the boxes of one kind of fruit. There will be 189 fruits in all. What kind of jam is she making?

   _____

3. If Mr. Melvin needs 50 apples for the school vending machines, will he be able to buy all of them from Mr. Dustin today? _____

4. How many apricots are on the truck? _____

Mr. Dustin's Harvest

Boxes of Fruit	Pieces of Fruit per Box
9 boxes of peaches	21 per box
5 boxes of pears	30 per box
2 boxes of apples	24 per box
3 boxes of apricots	52 per box

Honor Roll Luncheon

Multiplication With Regrouping

Name: _____

Date: _____

Sometimes, there is more than one way to find an answer.
You could use repeated addition to answer these questions, but multiplication is faster and more accurate.

> Diana and her friends made woven place mats for the Honor Roll Luncheon. For each place mat, they needed 6 strips of red paper and 9 strips of orange paper. They made 58 mats. They also made award certificates. On each certificate, they placed 7 gold stars and 5 silver stars. The certificates were awarded to 39 students.

1. How many strips of red paper did the girls use?

   _____

2. How many strips of orange paper did the girls use?

   _____

3. How many gold stars did they use? _____

4. If there were 200 silver stars in a box, was one box of silver stars enough, or did they open a second one? _____

Leggy Riddles

Division: One-Digit Divisor, No Remainder

Name: _____

Date: _____

For each problem, there are 72 legs. Use division to solve these leggy riddles.

1. Ladybird beetles each have six legs. How many ladybird beetles would there be? _____

2. Beagles have four legs each. How many beagles would there be? _____

3. With two legs each, how many basketball players would there be? _____

4. If there were two horses on a team, and all horses had four legs each, how many teams of horses would there be? _____

Bookstore Inventory

Division: One-Digit Divisor With Remainder

Name: _____

Date: _____

How would this bookstore divide up an important shipment? Read each question carefully. There will be remainders.

There are 89 books.

1. Copies of a best seller arrive at Downtown Books in 8 evenly-filled boxes. The remainder of the shipment is included in a padded envelope. How many books are in each box? _____ How many are in the envelope? _____

2. Most of the books are stored on two shelves in the back room. They are divided equally. How many books are on each shelf? _____
How many are left over? _____

3. Exactly nine books are sold each day. On which day is the last full batch of nine books sold: the eighth day, the ninth day, or the tenth day? _____

4. How many books are left on the last day? _____

Service Club

Division: One-Digit Divisor, Three-Digit Dividend, No Remainder

Name: _____

Date: _____

Read the paragraph and divide to answer the questions.

Two hundred pieces of trash were collected in Mason Park on Saturday morning. Eight service club members collected all of the litter. Each member collected the same number of pieces.

1. How many pieces of trash did each member collect?

   _____

2. Equal amounts of trash were placed in four plastic bags. How many pieces of trash were placed in each bag? _____

3. Equal amounts of trash were carried to the dump in two vans. How many pieces of trash were carried in each van? _____

4. The club earned one service point for each five pieces of trash collected. How many service points did the club receive? _____

Family Night Promotion

Division: One-Digit Divisor, Three-Digit Dividend With Remainder

Name: _____

Date: _____

Sometimes, remainders can answer questions. Solve these division problems.

Adventure Park wanted to promote Thursday as Family Night. They printed up 1,735 coupons good for one free game of kids' mini golf with the purchase of one adult game of mini golf.

1. Adventure Park mailed each family 3 coupons. How many families got coupons?

   _____

2. How many coupons were left over? _____

3. 107 families used all three coupons. How many coupons were used by these families? _____

4. 282 families used two of the three coupons. How many coupons were used by these families? _____

5. 96 families used only one coupon. How many coupons were used by these families? _____

6. Of those coupons mailed, how many coupons were not used? _____

Sports Card Collection

Checking Division With Multiplication

Name: _____

Date: _____

An easy way to check a division problem is to multiply the quotient by the divisor. If there is a remainder, add it to the product. The result should be the dividend.

When Jared organized his sports card collection, he realized he had duplicate cards. He decided to divide the 210 extra sports cards among five of his friends.

1. How many cards would each of his friends receive? _____

2. Before counting out the cards, Jared multiplied to be sure that he had divided them equally. Write the multiplication problem Jared used. _____

3. One of Jared's friends decided he did not want any cards, so Jared divided them into four sets instead. How many cards would be in each new set? How many would be left over? _____

4. Write the multiplication problem Jared used to check his division.

   _____

Recreation Organization

Division: Two-Digit Divisors

Name: _____

Date: _____

At the annual Founder's Day picnic, Mark and Jason helped the recreation director organize some activities. Divide to answer these questions.

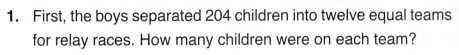

1. First, the boys separated 204 children into twelve equal teams for relay races. How many children were on each team?

   _____

2. Next, they prepared crafts materials. To assemble necklace kits, they divided 900 beads into sets with 25 beads each. How many kits did they make?

   _____

3. At lunchtime, they helped 180 children find their places at 15 tables. If the boys separated the children into equal groups, how many were seated at each table?

   _____

4. In the afternoon, Mark and Jason divided 170 children into 34 clusters for small-group nature activities. How many children were in each cluster?

   _____

Soccer Season

Averages

Name: _____

Date: _____

To find the average of a group of numbers, add them together, and then divide by the number of addends. For example, to find the average of 4, 2, and 3, add 4 + 2 + 3 = 9. Then divide 9 by 3, or 9 ÷ 3 = 3.

Kenneth's soccer team, the Westdale Tigers, played ten games during the season. Their scores are in the chart.

1. What was the average score in the first five games?

   _____

2. What was the average score in the second five games? _____

3. What was the average score in the last three games? _____

4. Did the team improve over the season or get worse?

   _____

Westdale Tigers Season Scores

Game	Score	Game	Score
Game 1	6	Game 6	4
Game 2	1	Game 7	4
Game 3	2	Game 8	3
Game 4	1	Game 9	5
Game 5	5	Game 10	4

Study Group

Averages

Name: _____

Date: _____

Check the facts and answer the questions.

Jake, Edgar, and Mark wanted to join the basketball team, but their grades were too low, so they formed a support group. For the first month, they helped each other study science and kept track of their scores.

	Jake	Edgar	Mark
Quiz 1	92	90	87
Quiz 2	89	92	88
Quiz 3	80	78	82
Quiz 4	92	84	83
Quiz 5	87	76	80

1. What was Edgar's average score for all five quizzes? _____

2. What was Mark's average score for all five quizzes? _____

3. What was the group's average score for Quiz 3? _____

4. What was the group's average score for Quiz 5? _____

5. Before forming the group, the boys' average quiz score was 64. Did they improve by Quiz 5? What was the boys' new average score for Quiz 5? _____

Two-Dimensional Geometry

Identifying Polygons, Lines, Line Segments, and Rays

Name: _____

Date: _____

A **line** is a collection of points extending in two directions with no end points. A **ray**, part of a line, has one endpoint. A **line segment** is part of a line with two endpoints. A **polygon** is a closed two-dimensional shape with three or more sides. Use these definitions and the diagrams to answer the questions.

Sengel Point lived on Planet Todimentia, an odd place where everything disappears if viewed from the side. One morning, Sengel could not find her sister, Ann Other.

1. First, she looked on the local line segment. Did she go to A, B, C, or D? _____

2. Next, she went to the polygon. Was it A, B, C, or D? _____

3. Ann was nowhere to be seen, so Sengel visited the line. Was it A, B, C, or D? _____

4. Finally, she found Ann on the ray. Was it A, B, C, or D? _____

Two-Dimensional Challenge

Identifying Polygons, Lines, Line Segments, and Rays

Name: _____

Date: _____

Here is a challenge! Use clues to name the homes of Todimentia's inhabitants. Circle the correct answer.

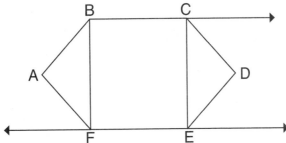

1. Dot Point's home is ABF. It is a (triangle / rectangle / hexagon).

2. Won Dot's home is FBCE. It is a (triangle / rectangle / hexagon).

3. A. Place lives on ABCDEF. It is a (triangle / rectangle / hexagon).

4. R. Spot is part of BC. It is a (polygon / line / ray).

5. Trudy Point lives on FE. That is a (triangle / line / line segment / ray).

Angles

Identifying Right Angles, Acute Angles, and Obtuse Angles

Name: _____

Date: _____

Acute angles are less than 90 degrees. **Right angles** are 90 degrees, and **obtuse angles** are greater than 90 degrees. Study the diagrams and circle the correct answers.

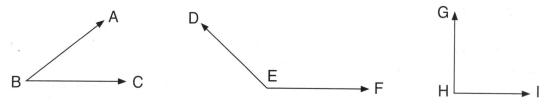

1. The shape of Lara's first initial is an angle. It is a(n) (right / acute / obtuse) angle.

2. When Charlie draws the profile of a bird, he uses an angle for the beak similar to ∠ABC. It is a(n) (right / acute / obtuse) angle.

3. When Mike draws a picture of his house, he uses an angle for the roof similar to ∠DEF. It is a(n) (right / acute / obtuse) angle.

4. A square has four angles. They are (right / acute / obtuse) angles.

Angle Names

Identifying Right Angles, Acute Angles, and Obtuse Angles

Name: _____

Date: _____

Angles have names. The letter in the middle labels the vertex. Each of the other letters labels a point on one of the sides. Study the diagram and circle the correct answers.

When Catherine drew a picture of her home's roof, she used many angles.

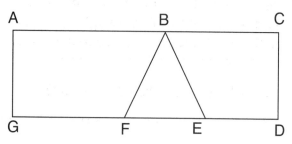

1. Angle BAG is a(n) (right / acute / obtuse) angle.

2. Angle FBE is a(n) (right / acute / obtuse) angle.

3. Angle BED is a(n) (right / acute / obtuse) angle.

4. How many acute angles are there in Catherine's picture? _____

5. How many obtuse angles are there in the picture? _____

6. How many right angles are there in the picture? _____

Sidewalk Chalk Circle

Identifying the Radius and Diameter of a Circle

Name: _____

Date: _____

The **radius** is a line segment connecting the center of a circle to a point on the circle. The **diameter** is a line segment that passes through the center of a circle and has both of its end points on the circle. The **circumference** is the perimeter of a circle. Study the diagram and answer the questions.

When Becky used sidewalk chalk to draw a foursquare court for her little sister, she labeled these points.

1. Is EB the radius, the diameter, or the

   circumference? _____

2. Is AC the radius, the diameter, or the

   circumference? _____

3. Is point E the center, the radius, or the circumference? _____

4. EC is one radius of this circle. Name three others. _____

Mystery Shape

Identifying the Radius and Diameter of a Circle

Name: _____

Date: _____

Jason drew a mystery shape with chalk. He told his brother to hold a broomstick very still. He tied one end of a piece of string to the broomstick and a piece of sidewalk chalk to the other end. He pulled the string tight and placed the chalk on the pavement. He kept the string tight and walked around the broomstick, drawing a line as he went.

1. What shape did Jason draw? _____

2. Was the straight piece of string a side, an angle, a radius, a diameter,

   or a circumference? _____

3. Every person in your class is standing exactly the same distance

   from you. What is the shape created by the other people, and what is the name of the spot

   where you are standing? _____

4. If a computer started to draw all the possible diameters of a circle, how many would there

   be? _____

Symmetrical Letters
Symmetry

After answering the questions, try cutting out some letters.

Anna is cutting out letters for a bulletin board. She has discovered that she can make some letters by folding and cutting. This is because some letters are symmetrical.

1. Circle the letters that are not symmetrical. On the symmetrical letters, draw lines to show planes of symmetry. These planes of symmetry will be Anna's fold lines. (Hint: Where would you place a mirror on half of the letter to make it look whole?)

A B C D E F G H I J K L M N O P Q R S T U V W X Y Z

2. When the gray areas are cut away, and the paper is unfolded, which letter will Anna see? _____

3. Draw a pattern for a folded letter Y in the box to the right. Color the cut-away section gray.

Logo Design
Symmetry

After answering the questions, design a symmetrical logo for your own website on your own paper.

Mark Matthews is designing a personal logo for his web site. The logo at right uses both of his initials. It has two planes of symmetry.

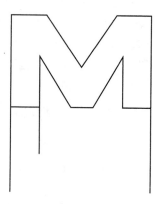

1. Finish Mark's logo.

2. Design a logo for Emily Ellenwood.

Congruent Covers
Identifying Congruent Figures

Name: _____
Date: _____

Congruent shapes may be turned, or oriented, in different directions, but they match in every other way. Study the diagrams and answer the questions.

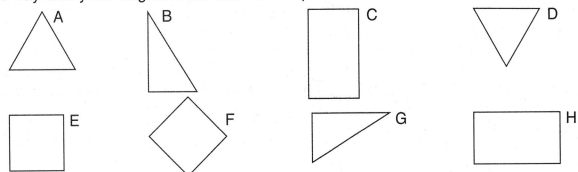

Jan, Kara, Jordan, and Martin are making shape books.

1. One of Jan's covers is A. What is her other cover? _____

2. Kara's covers are also triangles. Which ones are they? _____ , _____

3. One of Jordan's covers is H. What is the other? _____

4. One of Martin's covers is E. What is the other? _____

Spaceship Construction
Identifying Congruent Figures

Name: _____
Date: _____

Tony is assembling a spaceship control panel for his nephew. Metal pieces fit into special slots. Help Tony by identifying the congruent shapes. Study the panel and the pieces, and then answer the questions.

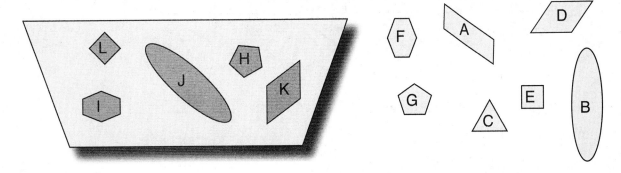

1. Which shape fits into slot J? _____   2. Which shape fits into slot L? _____

3. Which shape fits into slot K? _____   4. Circle the shapes that do not fit in the panel.

Eighth-Grade Facts

Identifying Fractions

Name: _____

Date: _____

The **numerator** (the top number in a fraction) tells how many parts are being described. The **denominator** (the number on the bottom) shows how many parts there are in all. Study the information below and answer the questions. Draw pictures on your own paper if you wish.

Abby is making a chart with information about Martin Junior High's eighth-grade class. She illustrates the following facts:

1. Abbie draws a circle divided into seven equal parts. How many of those parts does she color in? _____ Which fact is she illustrating? _____

2. Abbie draws a rectangle divided into six equal parts. How many of the parts does she color in? _____ Which fact is she illustrating? _____

3. Abbie draws a rectangle, divides it into equal parts, and colors in three of those parts. Which fact is she illustrating? _____

4. Abbie draws a circle, divides it into equal parts, and colors in seven of those parts. Which fact is she illustrating? _____

A. Seven-eighths of the students eat in the school cafeteria at least one day a week.

B. Five-sevenths of the students plan to attend college.

C. Three-fifths of the students enjoy athletic events.

D. Five-sixths of the students use the school library.

Fraction Detection

Identifying Fractions

Name: _____

Date: _____

Be a fraction detective. Use these clues to identify the items and write the fractions. Match the fraction diagrams to their descriptions.

A.

B.

C.

D.
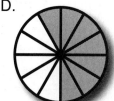
E.
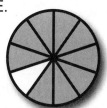

1. Seven green apples in a basket with five red apples _____

2. Two green chocolate buttons in a bowl with thirteen red chocolate buttons _____

3. Nine yellow pencils in a box with one blue pencil _____

4. Four white erasers in a drawer with thirteen gray erasers _____

5. Five red paper clips in a bag with four blue paper clips _____

Community Garden

Comparing Fractions Using a Fraction Bar Chart

Name: _____

Date: _____

Read the paragraph. Use the fraction bar chart to answer the questions.

Allen's class helped to plant a community garden. Each student was given a packet with the same number of seeds. Allen planted $\frac{9}{16}$ of his seeds. Grace planted $\frac{1}{2}$ of her seeds. Armando planted $\frac{4}{5}$ of his seeds, and Bill planted $\frac{5}{6}$ of his seeds.

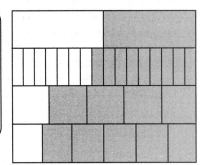

1. Who planted the most seeds? _____

2. Who planted the fewest seeds? _____

3. Who planted more seeds, Allen or Grace? _____

4. Who planted more seeds, Armando or Allen? _____

Challenge: Who ended the session with an equal number of planted and unplanted seeds?

_____

Filling Drink Cups

Recognizing Equivalent Fractions Using a Chart

Name: _____

Date: _____

Read the clues, and then write the girl's name and the fraction of cups she can fill across from the correct shaded bar. One has been done for you.

Name	Fraction
_____	_____
Carol	$\frac{4}{16}$
_____	_____
_____	_____
_____	_____

Carol and her friends are selling cold drinks at the game. Each girl has an identical pitcher and a stack of differently sized cups. A pitcher will fill 16 of Carol's cups, 12 of Anna's cups, and 10 of Laura's cups. A pitcher will also fill 6 of Geneva's cups, 4 of Mariah's, and 3 of Jamica's.

1. Carol filled 4 cups. That was $\frac{4}{16}$ of the lemonade in her pitcher. Anna used the same amount of lemonade. How many cups did she fill? _____

2. Laura filled five cups. That was $\frac{5}{10}$ of her lemonade. Mariah used the same amount of lemonade. How many cups did she fill? _____

Equivalent Fraction Contest

Name: _____

Date: _____

Generating Equivalent Fractions

Reminder: To create an equivalent fraction, multiply both the numerator and the denominator of a fraction by the same number.

Gabe, Kenyon, and Abe hold a contest. When Gabe says "go," the boys start writing equivalent fractions for $\frac{3}{4}$.

1. Kenyon likes to work in order. After $\frac{3}{4}$, he writes $\frac{6}{8}$. When Gabe says "stop," Kenyon is writing $\frac{30}{40}$. Fill in the blanks in Kenyon's list: $\frac{6}{8}$, _____, _____, _____, _____, _____, _____, _____, $\frac{30}{40}$.

2. Gabe likes to work in multiples of ten. After $\frac{3}{4}$, he writes $\frac{30}{40}$. When he says "stop," Gabe is writing $\frac{300}{400}$. Fill in the blanks in Gabe's list: $\frac{30}{40}$, _____, _____, _____, _____, _____, _____, $\frac{300}{400}$.

3. After $\frac{3}{4}$, Abe writes $\frac{15}{20}$. Then, he writes $\frac{30}{40}$, and then $\frac{45}{60}$. He continues to follow that pattern. What are his next two numbers? _____, _____

Trail Mix Recipe

Name: _____

Date: _____

Adding Fractions

When adding like fractions, add only the numerators. The denominators remain the same.

Many recipes use fractions. Read about Marlene's nut-free trail mix and answer the questions.

Marlene made nut-free trail mix for the class hike. The measuring cup she used was marked in 32nds. She included $\frac{7}{32}$ raisins, $\frac{10}{32}$ rice crackers, $\frac{5}{32}$ dried bananas, and $\frac{10}{32}$ pretzel pieces.

1. What fraction of the trail mix was sweet? _____

2. What fraction of the trail mix was salty? _____

3. What fraction of the trail mix did not include raisins? _____

4. What fraction of the trail mix did not include rice crackers? _____

Watermelon at the Picnic

Subtracting Fractions

Name: _____

Date: _____

Reminder: When subtracting like fractions, consider only the numerators. The denominators remain the same.

Read the paragraph and answer the questions in order.

At the town's SummerFest picnic, Ms. Carter cut a melon into 24 pieces and placed the slices on a serving table. Just as she finished, members of the dog parade group stopped by. They ate $\frac{11}{24}$ of the melon slices. Next, the volunteer firefighters arrived. They ate $\frac{10}{24}$ of the slices. After the firefighters left, Ms. Carter's children ate $\frac{2}{24}$ of the slices.

1. What fraction of the melon remained after the dog parade group left? _____

2. What fraction of the melon remained after the firefighters left? _____

3. What fraction of the melon remained after Ms. Carter's children finished snacking? _____

Computer Repair

Reducing Proper and Improper Fractions

Name: _____

Date: _____

To change an improper fraction to a mixed number, divide the numerator by the denominator. The quotient is the whole number, and the remainder is the numerator of the fraction part of the mixed number.

Read the example, and then fill in each missing mixed number.

Jacob fixes computer problems for customers on an hourly basis. He saves the money he earns for college. There are 60 minutes in an hour, so 90 minutes is the same as $\frac{90}{60}$ of an hour, or $1\frac{1}{2}$ hours.

1. 65 minutes = $\frac{65}{60}$ of an hour, or _____ hours.

2. 128 minutes = $\frac{128}{60}$ of an hour, or _____ hours.

3. 99 minutes = $\frac{99}{60}$ of an hour, or _____ hours.

4. 45 minutes = $\frac{45}{60}$ of an hour, or _____ hour.

Campground Rent

Changing Mixed Numbers to Improper Fractions

Name: _____

Date: _____

To change a mixed number to an improper fraction, multiply the whole number by the denominator, and add the numerator. The resulting number is the new numerator.

Waterfall Acres Campground is very popular. The owners charge visitors by the day and by any fraction of a day that they stay. There are 24 hours in a day, so 1 day and 2 hours is $\frac{26}{24}$ of a day. What fraction of a day are the following times?

1. 2 days and 4 hours = _____ of a day.

2. 1 day and 6 hours = _____ of a day.

3. 3 days and 1 hour = _____ of a day.

4. 1 day and 8 hours = _____ of a day.

Hiking the Trails

Adding and Subtracting Mixed Numbers

Name: _____

Date: _____

To add or subtract mixed numbers, keep the whole numbers lined up according to place value. If regrouping is necessary, remember that one whole equals a fraction with the same numerator and denominator.

1. On Saturday, Andy and David went on a hike. They packed $1\frac{1}{2}$ cheese and $1\frac{1}{2}$ chicken sandwiches. How many whole sandwiches did the boys take with them? _____

2. They walked $1\frac{1}{4}$ km and rested for 30 minutes. Afterwards, they walked another $1\frac{2}{4}$ km. They ate lunch beside a waterfall. Then, they walked back to the start of the trail. How far did they walk to get to the waterfall? _____
How far did they walk in all? _____

3. The boys were gone for $3\frac{3}{4}$ hours. They spent $1\frac{1}{4}$ hours eating lunch. How long did they spend walking? _____

4. It took the boys $1\frac{1}{2}$ hours to reach the waterfall. How long did it take them to hike back to the trailhead? _____ Which way do you think was uphill? Give a reason for your answer.

_____

Class Report Chart

Recognizing Decimal Fractions

Name: _____

Date: _____

Decimal fractions are based on multiples of ten.

Examples: The decimal fraction 0.1 is equal to the fraction $\frac{1}{10}$; $0.01 = \frac{1}{100}$; and $0.001 = \frac{1}{1000}$.

Sarah's committee created a chart for their class report. Sarah's job is to write a decimal fraction for each shaded part of each bar in the chart. Study the charts and write the decimal fractions.

1. _____

2. _____

3. _____

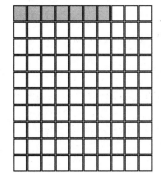

4. _____

Ordering Tile

Recognizing Decimal Fractions

Name: _____

Date: _____

Reminder: The decimal fraction 0.1 is equal to the fraction $\frac{1}{10}$; $0.01 = \frac{1}{100}$; and $0.001 = \frac{1}{1000}$.

Jason's father designs and installs tile floors. Last summer, Jason helped him write orders for tile. It was Jason's job to write the decimal fraction for the shaded part of each diagram. Write the decimal fractions below.

1.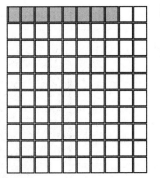

2.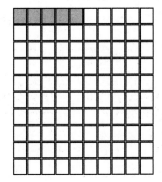

3.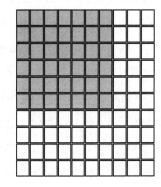

_____   _____   _____

Model Trains

Adding and Subtracting Decimal Fractions

Name: _____

Date: _____

Adding and subtracting decimal fractions is like any other addition or subtraction. Line up the decimal points according to place value.

Alden has model trains. He is putting together a freight train. The length of each car is listed in the table.

Type of Car	Length (in cm)
tank car	10.2
flat car	15.7
refrigerator car	13.4
caboose	7.6
engine	14.9

1. Alden adds only one of each type of car to his train. How long is it? _____

2. He adds three more tank cars to his train. Now how long is it? _____

3. The engine breaks down on the hill. Alden decides to remove the refrigerator car to lighten the load. Now how long is his train? _____

4. If he does some switching on his train and leaves the flat car on the side of the tracks, how long is his train now? _____

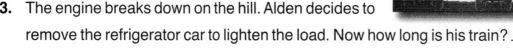

Book Weights

Adding and Subtracting Decimal Fractions

Name: _____

Date: _____

Reminder: Include the decimal point in your answer when adding or subtracting decimal fractions.

Book Title	Weight (in kg)
The Universe	1.81
Twenty Incredible Stories	1.94
Insects of the World	1.88
Endangered Animals	2.04

Gracie is putting books into her backpack. The pack's instructions warn not to carry more than 6.65 kilograms at once. The books Gracie wants to carry and how much they weigh are listed in the table.

1. If Gracie puts all of the books in her backpack, how much will it weigh? _____

2. How much over the pack's weight limit would that be? _____

3. If she removes *Twenty Incredible Stories*, how much would the remaining books weigh?

_____

4. If she puts *Twenty Incredible Stories* back in and removes *Endangered Animals* instead, how much would the remaining books weigh?

_____

Sharing Snacks

Comparing Decimals and Fractions

Name: _____

Date: _____

Reminder: When comparing decimals to fractions, 0.2 is the same as $\frac{2}{10}$ or $\frac{1}{5}$.

Carson and Danny are brothers. After a swim in the local pool, the boys go to the sandwich shop for a snack. Carson offers to give Danny a portion of his order. Danny is hungry, and he does not want his brother to trick him.

1. Should he choose $\frac{1}{2}$ or 0.4 of the sandwich? _____

2. Which should he choose, $\frac{1}{4}$ or 0.1 of the fries? _____

3. Should he choose $\frac{1}{6}$ or 0.6 of the drink? _____

4. Which should he choose, $\frac{2}{3}$ or 0.7 of the cookie?

   _____

5. Danny offers to pay $\frac{15}{30}$ or 0.5 of the bill. Which should Carson

   choose? _____

Votes for President

Comparing Decimals and Fractions

Name: _____

Date: _____

Reminder: 0.25 is the same as $\frac{25}{100}$ or $\frac{1}{4}$.

Rebecca wants to be the next student body president. Answer these questions about the votes she would like to get.

1. Would she rather receive 0.25 or $\frac{1}{3}$ of the boys' vote?

   _____

2. Would she rather receive 0.75 or $\frac{2}{3}$ of the girls' vote? _____

3. Would she rather receive 0.8 or $\frac{18}{20}$ of the seventh-grade vote? _____

4. Would she rather receive 0.67 or $\frac{7}{12}$ of the total vote? _____

Daily High Temperatures

Line Graphs

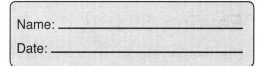

Name: _____

Date: _____

Study the graph and answer the questions.

1. What was the warmest day of the week?

_____

2. What were the coldest days of the week?

_____

3. How much warmer was it on Tuesday than

on Friday? _____

4. What was the average temperature for the

week? _____

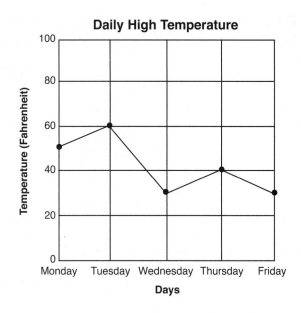

Daily High Temperature

Student Body Election

Bar Graphs

Name: _____

Date: _____

Study the graph and answer the questions.

1. Which candidate received the most votes?

_____

2. Which candidate received the fewest votes?

_____

3. How many more votes did Laura receive than

Denise? _____

4. How many votes were cast in all?

_____

5. What was the average number of votes

received per candidate? _____

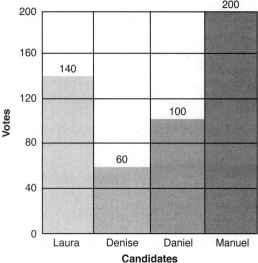

Student Body Election Results

Favorite Snacks

Pie Graphs

Pie graphs allow you to compare facts easily. The entire circle represents 100% of the results. Study the graph and answer the questions.

Favorite Snacks at Hillside School

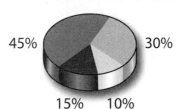

45%   30%

15%   10%

45% Prefer Apples
30% Prefer Bananas
10% Prefer Ants On A Log
15% Prefer Trail Mix

1. What is the favorite snack at Hillside School? _____

2. What is the least favorite snack? _____

3. The numbers on this graph represent percentages. If 100 students took the survey, how many of them chose apples? _____

4. How many more students preferred apples than preferred trail mix? _____

Coordinates on a Map

Ordered Pairs

Study the graph and answer the questions. In an ordered pair, the first number identifies the number of lines to the right (or left) of the vertex, and the second number identifies the number of lines above (or below) the vertex.

1. Jonathan's pet parakeet flew out the window. It flew to (1, 2). Where did it land?

    _____

2. Then it flew to (3, 4). On what did it land?

    _____

3. Next it flew to (4, 3). On what did it land?

    _____

4. What did it find at (5, 3)?

    _____

5. Jonathan finally found it at (4, 1). Was it beside a fence, in a park, or under a telephone pole?

    _____

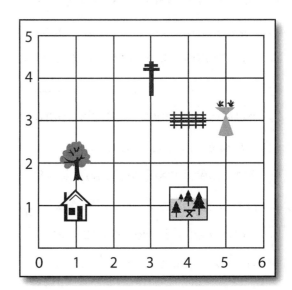

Picking a Gem

Probability

To find the probability of a certain outcome, compare the number of target items to the total number of items. Write the two numbers in this form: 5:10.

A velvet bag contains 10 gems. There are 4 sapphires, 3 diamonds, 2 emeralds, and 1 ruby. Reach into the bag and pull out a stone.

1. What is the probability of pulling out a ruby? _____

2. What is the probability of pulling out a sapphire? _____

3. What is the probability of pulling out an emerald? _____

4. What is the probability of pulling out a diamond? _____

5. What is the probability of not pulling out a ruby? _____

Challenge: Test the probability in real life! Use stones or marbles in place of the gems. Put the "gems" back and shake the bag after each draw.

Picking an Outfit

Tree Diagrams and Probability

Tree diagrams are a way to visualize possibilities. Use the information in the paragraph to label the diagram.

Casey has four shirts that are white, blue, tan, and yellow. She also has a pair of jeans, a pair of tan shorts, and a pair of denim shorts.

How many outfits can she make? Fill in the tree diagram to find out.

_____

If she picks her shirt and pants at random, what is her probability of choosing a blue shirt and tan shorts?

_____

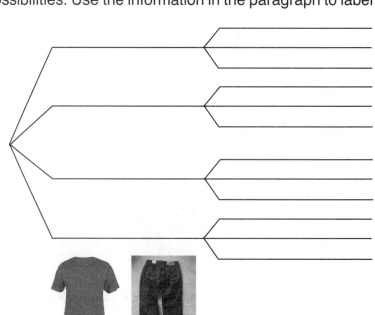

Building a Birdhouse

Measurement: Length—Inches, Feet, and Yards

Name: _____

Date: _____

Read about Jared's building project and answer the questions.

> Jared is making a birdhouse. The wood pieces for the front and back of the house should each be $7\frac{1}{2}''$ long. The wood piece for each of the two sides should be 6″ long.

1. If Jared wants his dad to cut all of the sides from one board, how many inches long must that board be?_____

2. The lumberyard measures boards in feet and inches. There are 12 inches in a foot. How many feet and inches long must the board be?

   _____

3. The lumberyard sells boards only in 4′, 6′, and 8′ lengths. Which board should Jared buy? _____

4. How long, in feet and inches, will the leftover piece be?

   _____

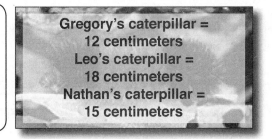

Caterpillar Race

Measurement: Length—Up to a Meter

Name: _____

Date: _____

Centimeters and meters are metric measurements. Metric measurements are based on multiples of ten. There are 100 centimeters in one meter.

> Gregory, Leo, and Nathan held a caterpillar race. They marked off the course in centimeters. The critter that traveled the farthest in three minutes would be the winner. When the race ended, the caterpillars had traveled the distances shown in the picture. (Note: All caterpillars were handled gently and released after the race.)

> Gregory's caterpillar = 12 centimeters
> Leo's caterpillar = 18 centimeters
> Nathan's caterpillar = 15 centimeters

1. How far did the winning caterpillar travel? _____

2. How far did the losing caterpillar travel? _____

3. What was the total distance traveled by all of the caterpillars? _____

4. What was the average distance traveled by the caterpillars? _____

5. If all three caterpillars continue to travel at the same rate for five more minutes, would their total distance in that five minutes equal one meter? _____

Wallpaper, Carpet, and Paint

Name: _____

Date: _____

Perimeter and Area

Perimeter is the distance around the outside of a shape. Area is the space that is contained within a shape. To find the perimeter of a rectangle, multiply the width by two and the length by two, and then add the results. To find the area of a rectangle, multiply the length by the width. Your answer will be in square units.

20′

16′

Becky is redecorating her room. She wants to buy a wallpaper border for the perimeter of her walls and carpet squares to cover the area of her floor. Her room is 16 ft. x 20 ft.

1. Each carpet square is 12 in. x 12 in. How many squares will Becky need for her room? _____

2. How many feet of the border will Becky need? _____

3. The border is measured in yards. How many yards will Becky need? _____

   20′

4. Becky wants to paint one of the long walls pale pink. To figure out how much paint to buy, Becky must know the area of the wall in square feet. If the wall is 8 feet tall and twenty feet long, what is its area in square feet? _____

   8′

Signs and Fences

Name: _____

Date: _____

Perimeter and Area

Reminder: Perimeter = (2 x length) + (2 x width)
              area = length x width.

Mathematicians use these shorthand formulas: $P = 2l + 2w$ and $A = lw$.

14 m

11 m

Jacob and Sam are helping prepare the park for the annual summer chess tournament.

1. The boys need to fence off the perimeter of an area that is 11 m long and 14 m wide. How many meters of fencing do they need? _____

2. What is the size of the fenced-off tournament area in square meters? _____

3. Next, the boys make a sign to hang near the entrance of the tournament area. It is 1 m high and 2 m long. How many square meters of paper do they use for the sign? _____

   2 m

   1 m

4. They glue a strip of red ribbon along the outside edges of the sign. How many meters of ribbon do they use? _____

Packaging Supplies

Volume

Name: _____

Date: _____

To find the volume of a solid, multiply the length times the width times the height, or $V = l \cdot w \cdot h$. Your answer will be in cubic units.

Ron's service club helped to pack boxes with donated supplies for schools damaged in a flood. Ron packed kindergarten building blocks into a box. Each block was 1 ft. long, 1 ft. tall, and 1 ft. wide. The box was 3 ft. long, 2 ft. tall, and 2 ft. wide.

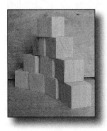

1. What was the size, in cubic feet, of each block? _____

2. How many blocks could Ron pack into the box? _____

3. There were still more blocks to pack, so Ron found another box. It was 4 ft. long, 2 ft. tall, and 1 ft. deep. How many blocks could he pack into that box? _____

4. After packing the second box, Ron still had 16 blocks left. Circle the box he should choose.

   A. a 2 ft. x 2 ft. x 2 ft. box   **B.** a 4 ft. x 4 ft. x 2 ft. box

   C. a 4 ft. x 2 ft. x 2 ft. box

Building a Raised Garden Bed

Metric Volume

Name: _____

Date: _____

The superscripted ^{3} stands for cubic units. For example, 3 m^3 means 3 cubic meters. Read the paragraph, and use the information to answer the questions. ***Reminder:*** $V = l \cdot w \cdot h$

Volunteers created a raised bed for a new garden at the botanical garden and planned to fill it with rich topsoil. The wooden bed they built was 40 cm deep, 85 cm long, and 90 cm wide.

1. How many cubic centimeters of topsoil would be needed to fill the container?

   _____

2. One cubic meter is 100 cm x 100 cm x 100 cm. How many cubic centimeters are there in one cubic meter? _____

3. If a farmer donated $\frac{1}{2}$ cubic meter (0.5 m^3) of clean topsoil, the volunteers would:

   A. have just enough soil.   **B.** have topsoil left over.   **C.** need more soil.

   Explain your answer. _____

4. The truck bed was 110 cm wide, 205 cm long, and 57 cm deep. How many cubic centimeters of soil could the farmer carry in one trip? _____

5. Would the farmer be able to deliver all of the soil at once, or would he need to make several trips? _____

Sports Equipment

Measurement: Weight—Ounces and Pounds

Name: _____

Date: _____

Ounces and pounds are common units of weight measurement used in America.

1. There are 16 ounces in a pound. Which balls weigh more than a pound? _____

2. A sports store ships 10 baseballs to a team's coach. How many ounces do the balls weigh? _____ How many pounds do they weigh? Write your answer as a mixed number. _____

Equipment	Approx. Weight
baseball	5 oz.
tennis ball	2 oz.
soccer ball	16 oz.
basketball	20 oz.

3. A sports team flew to a week-long training camp. They brought 5 balls with them. The balls weighed about 5 pounds. What kind of team was it? _____

4. Sweet Shot tennis balls come packed one pound per box. How many are there per box? _____

5. The gym coach bought a baseball, a tennis ball, a soccer ball, and a basketball. How much did his purchase weigh in ounces? _____ How much did it weigh in pounds? _____

An Elephant Diet

Measurement: Weight—Grams and Kilograms

Name: _____

Date: _____

Grams and kilograms are units of weight measurement in the metric system. A kilogram is equal to a thousand grams. Answer these weighty questions about elephants in the wild.

In the wild, an adult African elephant eats between 100 and 200 kg of vegetation each day.

1. If an elephant eats 112 kg of long grass, how many grams of grass has he eaten? _____

2. If an elephant eats 8,000 grams of fruit, how many kilograms of fruit has he eaten? _____

3. If an elephant eats 12 kg of baobab tree twigs, how many grams of wood has he eaten? _____

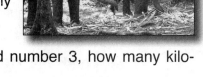

4. If an elephant eats everything in number 1, number 2, and number 3, how many kilograms of plant material has he eaten? _____

Taking the Ferry

Measurement: Weight—Kilograms and Metric Tons

Name: _____
Date: _____

Reminder: Add tags, such as km or g, to your answer.

The West Bay ferry can carry cars and trucks weighing a total of 236 metric tons.

Vehicle	Weight (in kg)
Car	1,200
Pickup	2,200
Van	2,800
Delivery truck	6,000

1. There are 1,000 kilograms in a metric ton. How many kilograms can the ferry safely carry? _____

2. What is the weight of 200 cars in kilograms? _____
   In metric tons? _____

3. What is the weight of 200 pickups in kilograms? _____
   In metric tons? _____

4. Can the ferry carry 200 cars? _____
   Can the ferry carry 100 cars and 50 pickups? _____

Challenge: What is the weight of one car, one pickup, one van, and one delivery truck in metric tons? _____

Camping Schedule

Elapsed Time

Name: _____
Date: _____

Tommy is going to summer camp for the first time. He wants to study the schedule so he knows what to expect. Each event begins as soon as the last one ends.

1. How long must campers wait from the end of breakfast to the beginning of lunch?

   _____

2. How long does the hike last?

   _____

3. How long do campers have to shower and dress in the morning?

   _____

4. How long is the lunch period?

   _____

5. How long is the morning meeting?

   _____

Program for Camp Blue Lake:

Tuesday Schedule:

Event	Time
Wake Up	7:00 AM
Breakfast	8:20 AM
Morning Meeting	9:05 AM
Hike	9:30 AM
Free Time	11:00 AM
Lunch	12:25 PM
Crafts	1:00 PM
Swimming	2:30 PM

Cycling for Charity

Speed and Distance

Reminder: 1 km = 1,000 m

During his first charity cycle ride, Stuart pedaled at a rate of 6 kilometers per hour. The checkpoints on the course are shown on the diagram.

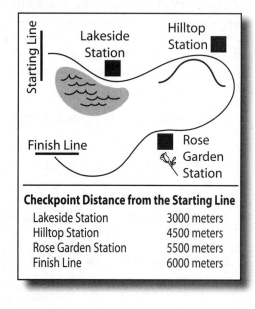

1. How long did it take Stuart to ride from the starting line to Lakeside Station?

    _____

2. How long did it take Stuart to ride from Hilltop Station to Rose Garden Station?

    _____

3. How long did it take Stuart to ride from the starting line to Hilltop Station? _____

4. How long did it take Stuart to ride the entire course? _____

Checkpoint Distance from the Starting Line	
Lakeside Station	3000 meters
Hilltop Station	4500 meters
Rose Garden Station	5500 meters
Finish Line	6000 meters

Canadian Time Zones

Time Zones

Use the map to count time zones and find the differences in time across the continent.
Reminder: A.M. means between midnight and noon; P.M. means between noon and midnight.
Subtract one hour for each time zone counted in a westerly direction.

1. If it is 6:00 A.M. in Edmonton, what time is it in Halifax? _____

2. If it is 9:00 P.M. in Toronto, what time is it in Edmonton? _____

3. If it is 7:00 P.M. in Halifax, what time is it in Winnipeg? _____

4. If it is 10:00 A.M. in Winnipeg, what time is it in Vancouver?

    _____

U.S. Money Facts

Money

Name: _____

Date: _____

Check the facts, and then answer these questions about money. On your own paper, explain how you found the answers.

1. If ten dimes are equal to $1, how many dimes are equal to $5? _____

2. If ten nickels are equal to $\frac{1}{2}$ dollar, how many nickels are equal to $10? _____

3. If four quarters are equal to $1, how many quarters are equal to $20? _____

4. If ten pennies are equal to a dime, how many pennies are equal to 50 dimes? _____

5. Write three different combinations of three different coins that equal the value of a half dollar.

   _____, _____, _____

Canadian Money Facts

Money

Name: _____

Date: _____

Check the facts, and then answer the questions about Canadian currency.

Canadian money has similar names and values to American money. The main difference is that Canada has a $1 coin, referred to as the "loonie," and a $2 coin, referred to as the "toonie."

| 0.01 penny | 0.05 nickel | 0.10 dime | 0.25 quarter | 1.00 dollar "loonie" | 2.00 two dollars "toonie" | 5.00 five dollar banknote |

1. 200 pennies are equal to a toonie, and ten pennies are equal to a dime. How many dimes are equal to a toonie? _____

2. 25 pennies are equal to a quarter, and 100 pennies are equal to a loonie. How many quarters are equal to a $5 banknote? _____

3. Two loonies are equal to one toonie. 40 nickels are equal to one toonie. How many nickels are equal to one loonie? _____

4. Write three different combinations of coins that equal one toonie.

   _____, _____, _____

Art Class

Money: Multiplying

Name: _____

Date: _____

Reminder: Do not forget the dollar signs and decimal points.

Jenny bought supplies for an after-school art class.

Item	Price per Item
Pad of paper	4.67
Tube of paint	2.99
Brush	3.25
Drawing pencil	1.05

1. How much did three pads of paper cost? _____
2. How much did 18 tubes of paint cost? _____
3. How much were 5 brushes? _____
4. How much were 12 pencils? _____
5. The shop was selling a prepackaged set of 12 pencils for $15.00. The set included a box that sold separately for $2.00. Was it a good buy? _____ Why or why not? _____

_____

6. At the end of the session, the class had a show. Jenny sold a drawing for $100. After expenses, how much did she earn? _____

Yard Care Company

Money: Dividing

Name: _____

Date: _____

Read the paragraph, and divide to answer these questions about a summer business partnership.

Christopher, Drew, Evan, Andres, and Benji formed a summertime yard care company. They agreed to work together on each project and to split their earnings equally. In the first week, they weeded Mrs. Cody's yard and earned $20.25. Next, they mowed Mr. Brian's yard and earned $6.50. They earned $5.20 for raking the leaves in Ms. Carson's yard, and $2.50 for sweeping Mrs. Amira's walkway. Finally, they planted Mr. Courtney's tomatoes, and he paid them $12.45.

1. How much did each boy earn for pulling Mrs. Cody's weeds? _____
2. How much did each boy earn for planting Mr. Courtney's tomatoes?

_____

3. How much did each boy earn for mowing Mr. Brian's lawn? _____
4. How much did each boy earn for his first week's work? _____
5. If each boy collected $137.40 for 12 weeks of work, how much did he earn per week?

_____

If each boy worked 5 hours per week, how much did he earn per hour? _____

Trip Destinations

Range, Median, and Mean

Name: _____

Date: _____

The **range** is the difference between the highest and lowest numbers in a group. The **median** is the number in the middle of the group of numbers when the numbers are arranged in order. If there are two numbers in the middle, the median is the average of those two numbers. The **mean** is the average of all of the numbers in a group.

Dustin took a poll to find out where students wanted to go on a school-sponsored trip.

Destination Votes

New York, NY	25
Washington, DC	14
London, England	30
Quebec City, Canada	26
Vancouver, Canada	20

1. What is the mean? _____
2. What is the median? _____
3. What is the range? _____
4. How many students responded to this poll?

   _____

5. There are 956 students at the school. How many did not respond? _____

Challenge: If you were a local business owner thinking about sponsoring a trip, how would this poll help you?

_____

Favorite TV Shows

Range, Median, and Mean

Name: _____

Date: _____

The **range** is the difference between the highest and lowest numbers in a group. The **median** is the number in the middle of a group of numbers when the numbers are arranged in order. If there are two numbers in the middle, the median is the average of those two numbers. The **mean** is the average of all of the numbers in a group.

Delinda took a poll on her blog to find out which television shows her readers were watching on Saturday nights.

Show	Number of Watchers
The Big Littles	254
Mark Anders, Middle School Detective	1,351
Talent Incorporated	2,194
From the Director's Chair	187
Dear Andrea	316

1. What is the mean? _____
2. Which shows have scores above the mean?

   _____

   _____

3. What is the median? _____
   Which show has the median score? _____
4. What is the range? _____ What does this tell you about the five shows? _____

5. How many people participated in the poll? _____

Challenge: How could advertisers use this information? Answer on your own paper.

Carpentry

Adding and Subtracting Unlike Fractions

Name: _____

Date: _____

Before adding or subtracting unlike fractions, you must change them to like fractions.

For Jake's first carpentry project, his dad helped him cut up four identical boards. He cut board A into thirds and board B into sixths. He cut board C into ninths and board D into twelfths. Divide the four boards as indicated and label each one. Then answer the questions below.

1. If Jake selected one piece of board A and one piece of board D, what fraction of a whole board would he have? _____

2. List at least two ways Jake could make $\frac{1}{2}$ of a board. _____ , _____

3. List at least two ways Jake could make $\frac{1}{3}$ of a whole board. _____ , _____

4. What could Jake add to four pieces of board D and three pieces of board C to equal the length of a whole board? _____

A.

B.

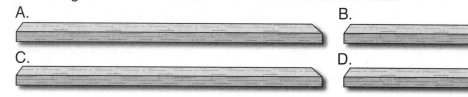

C.

D.

Pie Sale

Adding and Subtracting Mixed Numbers

Name: _____

Date: _____

When Sue visited the school fair at 3:00 P.M., three tables displayed pies for sale. On table A, there were $4\frac{1}{3}$ apple pies. On table B, there were $2\frac{5}{6}$ peach pies, and on table C, there were $1\frac{1}{12}$ cherry pies. Answer these questions about the pies.

1. If there were 10 apple pies at the beginning of the fair, how many were sold before Sue arrived?

    _____

2. How many more apple pies were left than cherry pies? _____

3. How many pies were left on the tables, in all?

    _____

4. How many peach and cherry pies were left?

    _____

Perimeter and Area of Figures

Multiplying Mixed Numbers

Name: _____

Date: _____

Before multiplying mixed numbers, change them to improper fractions. After multiplying, change them back to mixed numbers.

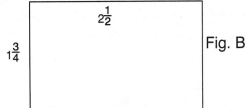

$\frac{1}{2}$ ☐ Fig. A

$\frac{1}{8}$

Fig. B

$2\frac{1}{2}$

$1\frac{3}{4}$

1. The sides of figure B measure $2\frac{1}{2}$ ft. x $1\frac{3}{4}$ ft. Find the perimeter. _____

2. Find the area of figure B. _____

3. The sides of figure A measure $\frac{1}{2}$ ft. x $\frac{1}{8}$ ft. Find the perimeter. _____

4. Find the area of figure A. _____

5. If figure A were attached to one side of figure B, what would the area of the new figure be?

_____

Perimeter and Area of a Room

Multiplying Mixed Numbers

Name: _____

Date: _____

Arthur's Room

Arthur's Bathroom

Arthur's Closet

Before multiplying mixed numbers, change them to improper fractions. After multiplying, change them back to mixed numbers.

1. Arthur's room is $14\frac{1}{2}$ ft. x $10\frac{1}{4}$ ft. Label the diagram. Find the perimeter._____

2. Find the area of Arthur's room. _____

3. Arthur's bathroom is $6\frac{1}{4}$ ft. x $5\frac{1}{2}$ ft. Label the diagram. Find the area. _____

4. Arthur's closet is $2\frac{1}{4}$ ft. x $6\frac{1}{4}$ ft. Label the diagram. Find the area. _____

5. What is the total area of Arthur's room, bathroom, and closet? _____

Computer Time

Dividing Fractions

Name: _____

Date: _____

To divide fractions, use the reciprocal of the divisor to multiply the dividend.

Example: $\frac{3}{4} \div \frac{2}{3} = \frac{3}{4} \times \frac{3}{2}$. Read the problems and answer the questions.

> Jake and his family share a new computer. Friday night is Jake's turn. He has $1\frac{1}{4}$ hours after dinner to use the machine.

1. On his first Friday night, Jake sent e-mails to his friends. If each e-mail took $\frac{1}{8}$ of an hour to finish, how many e-mails did he send? _____

2. On his second Friday night, Jake played his favorite computer game. If each level took $\frac{1}{2}$ of an hour to finish, how many levels did he complete? _____

3. On his third Friday night, Jake wrote movie reviews in his blog. If each review took $\frac{1}{3}$ of an hour to finish, how many reviews did he write? _____

4. On his fourth Friday night, Jake chatted with friends. If he chatted with each friend for $\frac{1}{4}$ of an hour, how many friends did he contact? _____

- -

Art Projects

Dividing Fractions

Name: _____

Date: _____

To divide fractions, use the reciprocal of the divisor to multiply the dividend.

Example: $\frac{3}{4} \div \frac{2}{3} = \frac{3}{4} \times \frac{3}{2}$. Read the problems and answer the questions.

> Mrs. Wilson, the art teacher, had a $6\frac{1}{2}$ square foot (sq. ft.) sheet of white paper.

1. She needed squares that were $\frac{3}{4}$ of a sq. ft. for a project. How many $\frac{3}{4}$ ft. squares could she cut from the $6\frac{1}{2}$ sq. ft. sheet of paper? _____

2. She decided to make the squares a little smaller. How many $\frac{1}{2}$ ft. squares could she cut from the $6\frac{1}{2}$ sq. ft. sheet? _____

3. Mr. Davis gave Mrs. Wilson a larger sheet of pale blue paper. It was $7\frac{3}{8}$ sq. ft. How many $\frac{1}{2}$ ft. squares could she cut from the blue paper? _____

4. Since she had more paper, Mrs. Wilson decided to make each square slightly larger. How many $\frac{5}{8}$ ft. squares could she cut from the $7\frac{3}{8}$ sq. ft. paper? _____

Keeping Track of Middle-Schoolers

Multiplying With Decimal Fraction Multipliers

Name: _____

Date: _____

To multiply a whole number by a decimal fraction, simply multiply as usual. The decimal must be in the same place in the product as it is in the multiplier.

Example:

```
    12
  x 0.2
  -----
   2.4
```

Students at Pleasant Valley Middle School

Grade	# of Students
6	170
7	140
8	160

1. Nine-tenths of the students in the seventh grade will be returning to Pleasant Valley Middle School next year. How many seventh-graders will be returning? _____ How many will not be returning? _____

2. Five-hundredths of the students in the eighth grade will be attending an honors high school program. How many of the eighth-graders will be part of the program? _____

3. Two-tenths of the students in the sixth grade will sign up for the school service club. How many sixth graders will sign up? _____

4. Three-tenths of the seventh-graders are already in the club. How many seventh-graders are in the school service club? _____

Fundraising

Multiplying With Decimal Fraction Multipliers

Name: _____

Date: _____

To multiply a whole number by a decimal fraction, simply multiply as usual. The decimal must be in the same place in the product as it is in the multiplier.

Example:

```
    12
  x 0.2
  -----
   2.4
```

1. Five-hundredths of the money raised in 2012 was used for postage. How much was spent on postage? _____

2. Three-thousandths of the money raised in 2013 was used to buy lightbulbs for the office. How much was spent on lightbulbs? _____

3. Six-tenths of the money raised in 2014 was used to support the food bank. How much money was used to support the food bank? _____

4. Four-tenths of the money raised in 2015 was used to support the Clothing Exchange Shop. How much money was used to support the Clothing Exchange Shop?

_____

MONEY RAISED FOR COMMUNITY HOPE

YEAR	DOLLARS
2012	$3,295
2013	$4,255
2014	$2,600
2015	$3,540

Lemonade Fill-Up

Dividing With Decimal Fraction Divisors

Name: _____

Date: _____

Before dividing by a decimal fraction, you can multiply both the divisor and the dividend by ten, one hundred, or one thousand to eliminate the decimal point in the divisor.

Example: 9.3 ÷ 3.1   9.3 x 10 = 93   3.1 x 10 = 31   93 ÷ 31 = 3

Divide to answer the questions. Round decimal fractions to the nearest hundredth if necessary.

> Cynthia had 6.5 liters of lemonade.

1. How many 0.25-liter cups of lemonade could she fill?

   _____

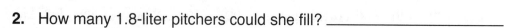

2. How many 1.8-liter pitchers could she fill? _____

3. How many 0.95-liter hiker's bottles could she fill? _____

4. How many 0.35-liter glasses could she fill? _____

Cancer Fundraiser

Dividing With Decimal Fraction Divisors

Name: _____

Date: _____

Before dividing by a decimal fraction, you can multiply both the divisor and the dividend by ten, one hundred, or one thousand to eliminate the decimal point in the divisor. Divide to answer the questions. Round decimal fractions to the nearest hundredth if necessary.

> Regina's mother is a cancer survivor, so Regina is raising money for cancer research. A sewing shop donated 5.05 meters of pink ribbon.

1. Pink bow pins for the cancer awareness campaign take 0.20 meters of ribbon each. How many pink bows could Regina make with the ribbon? _____

2. Wrapping gifts for cancer patients in the hospital takes 0.82 meters of ribbon per gift. How many gifts could Regina wrap? _____

3. Making necklaces for the group's gift shop takes 0.65 meters of ribbon per necklace. How many necklaces could Regina make? _____

4. Pink ribbon refrigerator door magnets take 0.05 meters of ribbon per magnet. How many magnets could Regina decorate? _____

Basketball Percentages

Percents

Name: _____

Date: _____

Percent means "portion of a hundred." To find the percentage, divide the target number by the total possible.

Example: 10 out of 100 is $\frac{10}{100}$, which is the same as 0.10, or 10%.

Round the answers to the nearest percent.

1. What percentage of baskets did Ken score in August? _____

2. What percentage of baskets did Javier score in August? _____

3. What percentage of baskets did Graham score in August? _____

4. What percentage of baskets did Leo score in August? _____

5. Which player sank the greatest percentage of baskets in August? _____

Basketball Practice August

	Baskets	Shots
Ken	40	152
Javier	83	194
Graham	76	99
Leo	92	105

Rose Garden

Ratios

Name: _____

Date: _____

Ratios compare numbers. They are written in this form: 12:2.

The West Valley Botanical Gardens has a beautiful rose garden. There are 25 red roses, 50 pink roses, 15 yellow roses, and only 10 white roses.

1. The ratio of red roses to pink roses is 25: _____, 50: _____, or 100: _____.

2. The ratio of white to yellow roses is _____ :15, 20: _____, or 30: _____.

3. The ratio of pink roses to white roses is 50: _____, 5: _____, or

   100: _____.

4. The ratio of yellow roses to red roses is 15:

   _____, 30: _____, or _____ :100.

Scale Models

Proportions

Name: _____

Date: _____

A ratio can also be written as a fraction. To find an unknown number in a pair of ratios, cross-multiply. For example, $\frac{2}{3} = \frac{?}{6}$. The missing number is 4 because 2 x 6 = 12 and 3 x 4 = 12.

Jake constructs scale model buildings for the town museum. He measures the Old Town Hall carefully to make his model as accurate as possible. Jake uses two centimeters to represent each meter in his model.

1. How long will each of the miniature town hall's sides be? 2 cm/1 m = _____ cm/20 m

2. How wide will the model building be?
   2 cm/1 m = _____ cm/15 m

3. How wide will the model's front door be?
   2 cm/1 m = _____ cm/2 m

4. How tall will the model's front door be?
   2 cm/1 m = _____ cm/3 m

Measurements of the Old Town Hall

Building Part	Measurement in Meters
Length of each side	20
Length of front and back	15
Width of front door	2
Height of front door	3

Expanding Recipes

Proportions

Name: _____

Date: _____

A ratio can also be written as a fraction. To find an unknown number in a pair of ratios, cross-multiply. For example, $\frac{2}{3} = \frac{?}{6}$. The missing number is 4 because 2 x 6 = 12 and 3 x 4 = 12.

Anna and Christina are preparing refreshments for a summer pool party.

1. For every measuring cup of punch mix, they are directed to use 6 measuring cups of water. Each measuring cup is about one serving, and the girls want to make 42 servings.

   How many cups of punch mix should they use? $\frac{1}{6} = \frac{}{42}$

For each two pizza snacks, they will need 1 English muffin, 2 oz. canned pizza sauce, two slices of cheese, and six slices of pepperoni.

2. How many English muffins will they need if they want to make 20 pizza snacks?
   $\frac{1}{2} = \frac{}{20}$

3. How many ounces of canned pizza sauce will they need? $\frac{2}{2} = \frac{}{20}$

4. How many slices of pepperoni will they need? $\frac{6}{2} = \frac{}{20}$

3-D Objects in a Flat World

Three-Dimensional Forms

Name: _____

Date: _____

In a world with only two dimensions, how would three-dimensional objects appear?

(In Flatworld, there are only two dimensions.)

1. When lying down, this Flatworld character looks like either a point floating in space or a circle, but, when standing, he looks like a triangle. In our world, what three-dimensional shape would he be? _____

2. When lying down, this Flatworld character looks like a square. Actually, when seen from any of his six faces, this fellow looks exactly the same. In our world, what three-dimensional shape would he be? _____

3. When lying down, this Flatworld character looks like either a square or a point floating in space, but, when standing, he looks like a triangle. In our world, what three-dimensional shape would he be? _____

4. From any angle, this Flatworld character looks like a circle. In our world, what three-dimensional shape would he be? _____

5. What would a cylinder look like in Flatworld? Why? _____

- -

Detecting 3-D Objects

Three-Dimensional Forms

Name: _____

Date: _____

Dimensional Detective Work

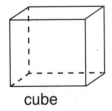

cube   square pyramid   triangular prism

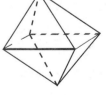

octahedron

1. I have 12 edges, 8 vertices, and all 6 of my faces are congruent.
   What am I? _____

2. I have 8 edges, 5 vertices, and only one of my 5 faces is square.
   What am I? _____

3. I have 12 edges, 6 vertices, and all of my eight faces are triangular.
   What am I? _____

4. I have 9 edges and 6 vertices. I also have five faces. Three of them are quadrilaterals, and two are triangles. What am I? _____

Making Circles

Circumference

Name: _____

Date: _____

Find the circumference of a circle by multiplying the radius by 2 and then multiplying the result by pi (π). For this exercise, round π off to the nearest hundredth (3.14).

Denise is making some signs for the spring dance. The theme is "Bubbles." She wants to glue heavy black yarn around the edges of different sizes of cardboard circles, but she needs to know how much yarn to buy.

1. The red circle has a radius of 30 cm. How much yarn does Denise need for the circumference? _____

2. The yellow circle has a radius of 20 cm. How much yarn does Denise need for the circumference? _____

3. The green circle has a radius of 45 cm. How much yarn does Denise need for the circumference? _____

4. The blue circle has a radius of 40 cm. How much yarn does Denise need for the circumference? _____

5. How much yarn does she need in all? _____

Ring Around the Horses

Circumference

Name: _____

Date: _____

Find the circumference of a circle by multiplying the radius by 2 and then multiplying the result by pi (π). For this exercise, round π off to the nearest hundredth (3.14).

Mark is helping his uncle build a fence around the exercise ring at his horse ranch.

1. The outer ring has a radius of 25 meters. How many meters of fencing will they need? _____

2. The inner ring will also need a special, lower fence. It has a radius of 6 meters. How much of the lower fencing will they need?

   _____

3. After they finish building the fences, Mark and his uncle will place circles of wire fencing around the bases of some young apple trees to protect their bark from grazing deer. The circle of wire around each trunk will have a radius of 25 cm. How much wire fencing will they need for each tree? _____

Challenge: If Mark stands in the ring holding a rope, and a tethered horse trots around him in a circle with a circumference of 18.84 m, how long is the rope? _____

Painting Triangles

Areas of Triangles

Name: _____

Date: _____

To find the area of a triangle, multiply $\frac{1}{2}$ times the base times the height, or $A = \frac{1}{2} bh$. Read the

paragraph, and then answer the questions.

Jackie and Ellen want to have a large triangle painted on the wall of the recreation center. They need to know the number of square feet there will be in the triangle so they can order the correct amount of paint.

1. If the triangle has a base of 12 ft. and a height of 10 ft., how many square feet will it cover?

   _____

2. If the triangle has a base of 16 ft. and a height of 12 ft., how many square feet will it cover?

   _____

3. If the triangle has a base of 10 ft. and a height of 6 ft., how many square feet will it cover? _____

4. If the triangle has a base of 20 ft. and a height of 16 ft., how many square feet will it cover? _____

Birdwatching Shelter

Areas of Complex Shapes

Name: _____

Date: _____

To find the area of a complex shape, find the area of each section, and then total the areas of the sections.

The floor plan for the botanical garden's new birdwatching shelter is made up of three parts. The main shelter is 12 ft. x 6 ft. The height of the triangular section is 4 ft. A small rectangular entryway is 6 ft. x 3 ft. Label each part of the drawing, and then answer the questions.

1. What is the area of the main shelter?

   _____

2. What is the area of the triangular section?

   _____

3. What is the area of the entryway?

   _____

4. What is the area of the entire shelter?

   _____

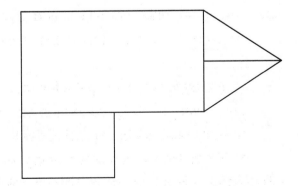

Insect Populations

Pictographs

Name: _____

Date: _____

In a pictograph, each picture stands for a certain amount. Study the chart and answer the questions.

Jana surveyed the insects in her yard. In the pictograph, each insect represents 7 insects she counted.

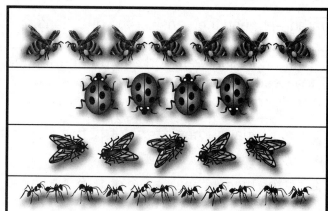

1. How many ants did she count?

    _____

2. How many more flies did she count than ladybugs? _____

3. How many more bees did she count than ladybugs? _____

4. How many insects did Jana count? _____

5. What was the ratio of ants to flies? _____

6. What was the proportion of ladybugs to flies? _____/5 = 28/_____

School Desk Inventory

Pictographs

Name: _____

Date: _____

In a pictograph, each picture stands for a certain amount. Study the chart and answer the questions.

At the end of the school year, Mrs. Kramer took inventory of her desk. Each symbol represents 15 items.

1. How many paper clips were in Mrs. Kramer's desk?

    _____

2. How many tacks were in Mrs. Kramer's desk?

    _____

3. How many more pencils than paper clips were there? _____

4. What was the ratio of tacks to paper clips?

    _____

5. How many items were in Mrs. Kramer's desk?

    _____

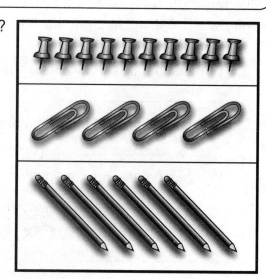

Decoding a Message

Coordinate Graphing

Name: _____

Date: _____

In an ordered pair, the first number tells how many points to move horizontally on the grid and the second number tells how many points to move vertically.

> A coded message arrived at headquarters. It is the missing character in a password. Decode the message by marking the location of each ordered pair on the grid.

1. Place a dot at (4, 4). Place a dot at (-4, -4). Draw a line connecting those two dots

2. Place a dot at (-4, 4) and a dot at (4, -4). Draw a line connecting those two dots.

   What is the missing character? _____

Challenge: On your own grid, draw a polygon, and place points at each of the vertices. Describe the position of each of the points with an ordered pair. Write directions to solve, and invite a partner to recreate your polygon.

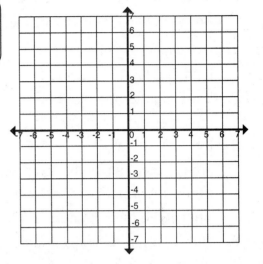

Soccer Spectators

Logic Problems

Name: _____

Date: _____

On your own paper, draw a diagram to solve this logic problem.

> Five friends were watching a soccer match. They were the only ones sitting in that row of the bleachers. Becky was sitting to the right of Jake. Carol was not sitting next to Tom. Brian was not sitting next to Jake. Tom was sitting to the right of Brian. Carol was not sitting next to Jake or Brian.

1. Who was sitting next to Carol? _____

2. Tom was sitting on one side of Brian. Who was sitting on the other side?

   _____

3. Which two friends were on the ends of the bench? _____

4. Which boy was sitting next to Jake? _____

5. Who was sitting in the middle? _____

Temperature Changes

Integers

Name: _____

Date: _____

Integers include whole numbers above and below 0 on the number line. **Negative integers** are commonly used in accounting, time lines, and in temperature readings.

Reminder: A positive times a positive is a positive, and a negative times a negative is a positive.

1. If a winter day has a high of 10°C and a low of -15°C, what is the difference between the high and low? _____

2. If the high temperature is -1°C, and the low temperature is -18°C, what is the difference between the high and low? _____

3. If the temperature was -2°C at 5:30 A.M., but it is 18°C at 12:30 P.M., how many degrees has the temperature risen? _____

4. If the temperature is -5° at 6:00 A.M., and it rises 14°C to hit its high at 1:15 P.M., what is the high temperature for the day? _____

5. If the daytime high on January 10 was -5°C, and the daytime high on July 10 was 30°C, how many times hotter was it on the July day? _____

Wrapping Boxes

Surface Area of Rectangular Solids

Name: _____

Date: _____

To find the surface area of a three-dimensional rectangular form, find the area of each surface and add the products together.

Box 2

19" l x 17" w x 14" h

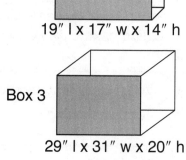

| Jenny made props for a play. She wanted to cover several rectangular boxes with gift wrap. How many square inches of wrapping paper does she need? |

Box 1

26" l x 15" w x 18" h

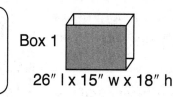

Box 3

29" l x 31" w x 20" h

1. Find the surface area of each box.

   Box 1: _____ Box 2: _____

   Box 3: _____ Box 4: _____

2. Find the total surface area for all four boxes.

   _____

Box 4

32" l x 16" w x 22" h

3. Opposite sides of a rectangular form are congruent. Can you think of a shortcut to find the surface area? _____

Savings Account

Calculating Interest

Name: _____

Date: _____

Use your knowledge of percents to answer these questions about Jared's savings account. At the end of the year, the interest is added to the total in the account.

1. Jared has $350 in his account. On January 2, his uncle gives him $210 to deposit. How much money does Jared have in his account now?

   _____

2. Jared does not deposit any more money, but his money does earn 4% interest per year. How much interest does it earn during the year? _____

3. How much money does Jared have at the end of the year? _____

4. Jared's father matches the money in Jared's account at the end of the year. After his father's deposit, how much money is in Jared's account? _____

5. The bank raises its interest rate to 5% per year. How much interest will Jared earn on his growing account during the next year? _____

Class Can Collection

Multiple Line Graphs

Name: _____

Date: _____

Study the graph and answer the questions.

1. How many total cans did all of the classes collect during week one? _____

2. Which class started poorly and improved?

   _____

3. Which class brought in the most cans?

   _____

4. Which classes' contributions had a mode of 10 cans? _____

5. Which class had a mean contribution of 22 cans? _____

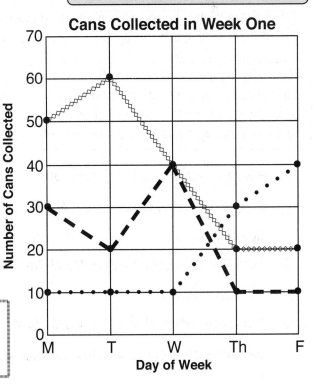

Cans Collected in Week One

· · · · · Class One
◇◇◇◇◇◇◇ Class Two
━ ━ ━ Class Three

Confused Equations

Equations With Missing Operations

Thieves entered Algebraica during the night and stole all of the operations signs. In the morning, all of the equations were confused. Help them out by adding all of the missing signs. Each sign is used only once. They are +, −, x, ÷, >, <, and =.

1. 12 _____ $42 = 504$

2. $1{,}836$ _____ $36 = 51$

3. 82 _____ $87 = 169$

4. $10{,}892$ _____ $8{,}211 = 2{,}681$

5. $223 + 74$ _____ $122 + 91$

6. 12×14 _____ $100 + 90$

7. $72 \div 12$ _____ 6×1

Carnival Prize

Venn Diagrams

Andy went to the carnival. There were three overlapping plastic hoops in one of the booths. In each section, there were numbers. The barker at the booth said Andy could win a prize if he picked the right ring. When all of the numbers in that ring were multiplied together, the product would be a number with three digits. When the digits of that answer were added together, their sum would equal 4. Andy won!

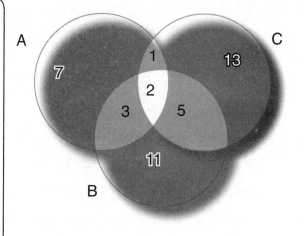

1. Which ring did he choose? _____

2. What was the smallest product of the numbers in the rings? _____

Birthday Riddle

Exponents

Exponents tell you how many times to multiply a number by itself.

Example: 5 x 5 x 5 is 5^3.

> Danny's mother had a birthday party yesterday. Danny asked her how old she was, and she hesitated.

1. Finally, she said that she was 2^5 years old. How old was she?

    _____

2. Danny's older brother said he was 2^4 years old. How old was he? _____

3. Danny's younger brother said he was 3^2 years old. How old was he? _____

4. If Danny is $2^3 + 2^2$ years old, how old is he? _____

Reunion Leftovers

Reducing Fractions

Reducing fractions to their lowest terms sometimes takes several steps. To save time, find the greatest common factor for the numerator and denominator. Multiplication practice will help you recognize factors more quickly. Read the questions and reduce the fractions to their lowest terms.

> After the family reunion, Andy helped his cousin gather up the food remaining on the tables.

1. Originally, there had been 144 chocolate chip cookies. There were 16 chocolate chip cookies left, or $\frac{16}{144}$ of the total. Reduce the fraction to its lowest terms. _____

2. There were 49 butter cookies left. Originally, there had been 98 butter cookies. $\frac{49}{98}$ were left. Reduce the fraction to its lowest terms. _____

3. Originally, there were 160 oz. of punch. The boys found that 32 oz. of punch were left. That was $\frac{32}{160}$, or _____.

4. Originally, there had been 125 paper cups. When the boys put the remaining cups back into the box, they found 50. That was $\frac{50}{125}$, or _____.

Fractions and Calculators

Changing Fractions to Decimals

Name: _____

Date: _____

To change a fraction to a decimal, divide the numerator by the denominator.

1. Jake wanted to check some fraction problems with his calculator, but when he tried, he discovered that the device showed only decimals. To check his answers, he had to change each fraction into a decimal. His first answer was $\frac{5}{12}$. How would $\frac{5}{12}$ appear on his calculator screen? Round off the result to the nearest thousandth. _____

2. What was special about the number? _____
_____

3. Which is a more exact representation of the quantity, $\frac{5}{12}$ or 0.417? _____
Give a reason for your answer. _____

4. What are the advantages of using decimal fractions? _____
_____

- -

Finding Prime Factors

Factor Trees

Name: _____

Date: _____

Jan made a factor tree to find the prime factors for 192. Unfortunately, she left her paper on the patio, and some of the numbers were washed away.

1. Write the missing numbers on the diagram.

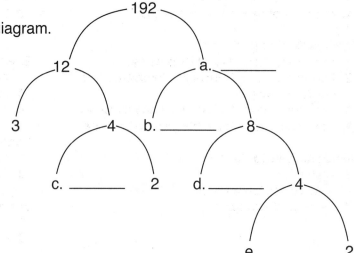

2. List the prime factorization of 192.

_____

Answer Keys

Marine Biology (p. 1)
1. 4 lines: 62 in line 1, 60 in line 2, 56 in line 3, 59 in line 4
2. spiny lobsters
3. Answers will vary.
4. Answers will vary.

Organic Gardening (p. 1)
1. row 2
2. 12 pepper plants
3. 17 corn plants
4. 5 watermelon plants
5. She grew more beefsteak tomatoes.

Recycling Drive (p. 2)
1. 995 cans
2. 1,152 cans
3. 1,344 cans
4. 885 cans
5. Jeremy and Jordan

Arachnid Research (p. 2)
1. 262 spiders
2. 281 spiders
3. 293 spiders
4. 370 spiders

Library Returns (p. 3)
1. 278 books
2. 128 books
3. 118 books
4. 468 books

Recycling Plastics (p. 3)
1. 104 bottles
2. 38 bottles
3. 97 bottles
4. 30 bottles

Food Bank Inventory (p. 4)
1. 237 cans of garbanzo beans
2. 1,018 cans of beans
3. 103 cans of black beans
4. 818 cans of navy and black beans

Farmers Market (p. 4)
1. *How many more, than,* 129 tomatoes
2. *How many, in all,* 635 onions, tomatoes, and cilantro bunches
3. *How many, in all,* 399 potatoes and tomatoes
4. *How many more, than,* 209 cilantro bunches

Demographics (p. 5)
1. *Lady's Life*
2. a men's golf tournament
3. the boys' department

Waterfalls (p. 5)
1. Angel Falls and Tugela Falls
2. Tugela Falls and Monge Falls
3. Tugela Falls
4. 9,000 ft.

Fruit Harvest (p. 6)
1. 150 pears
2. peach jam
3. no
4. 156 apricots

Honor Roll Luncheon (p. 6)
1. 348 strips of red paper
2. 522 strips of orange paper
3. 273 gold stars
4. They used 195 silver stars, so one box of 200 was enough.

Leggy Riddles (p. 7)
1. 12 ladybird beetles
2. 18 beagles
3. 36 basketball players
4. nine teams of horses

Bookstore Inventory (p. 7)
1. 11 books in each box and 1 book in the envelope
2. 44 books per shelf with 1 left over
3. the ninth day
4. 8 books left

Service Club (p. 8)
1. 25 pieces of trash
2. 50 pieces of trash
3. 100 pieces of trash
4. 40 points

Family Night Promotion (p. 8)
1. 578 families
2. 1 coupon
3. 321 coupons
4. 564 coupons
5. 96 coupons
6. 753 coupons

Sports Card Collection (p. 9)
1. 42 cards
2. 42 x 5 = 210
3. 52 cards with 2 left over
4. 52 x 4 = 208 + 2 = 210

Recreation Organization (p. 9)
1. 17 children
2. 36 kits
3. 12 children
4. 5 children

Soccer Season (p. 10)
1. 3 points
2. 4 points
3. 4 points
4. improve

Study Group (p. 10)
1. 84   **2.** 84
3. 80   **4.** 81
5. Yes, their average score on Quiz 5 was 81.

Two-Dimensional Geometry (p. 11)
1. D   **2.** A
3. B   **4.** C

Two-Dimensional Challenge (p. 11)
1. triangle   **2.** rectangle
3. hexagon   **4.** ray
5. line

Angles (p. 12)
1. right   **2.** acute
3. obtuse   **4.** right

Angle Names (p. 12)
1. right   **2.** acute
3. obtuse   **4.** 5
5. 2   **6.** 4

Sidewalk Chalk Circle (p. 13)
1. radius   **2.** diameter
3. center   **4.** ED, EA, and EB

Mystery Shape (p. 13)
1. a circle   **2.** a radius
3. The shape is a circle, and you are in the center of the circle.
4. an infinite number

Symmetrical Letter (p. 14)
1. A̶ B̶ C̶ D̶ E̶ H̶ I̶ M̶ O̶ T̶ U̶ V̶ W̶ X̶ Y̶
2. H
3.

Logo Design (p. 14)
1.
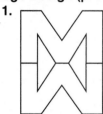

2. Answers will vary. Should include two Es. Students' own designs will vary.

Congruent Covers (p. 15)
1. D   **2.** B and G
3. C   **4.** F

Spaceship Construction (p. 15)
1. B   **2.** E
3. D   **4.** A and C do not fit.

Eighth-Grade Facts (p. 16)
1. five, B   **2.** five, D
3. C   **4.** A

Fraction Detection (p. 16)
1. D   **2.** A
3. E   **4.** C
5. B

Community Garden (p. 17)
1. Bill   **2.** Grace
3. Allen   **4.** Armando
Challenge: Grace

Filling Drinking Cups(p. 17)
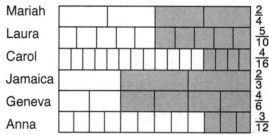

1. 3
2. 2

Equivalent Fraction Contest (p. 18)
1. $\frac{9}{12}, \frac{12}{16}, \frac{15}{20}, \frac{18}{24}, \frac{21}{28}, \frac{24}{32}, \frac{27}{36}$

2. $\frac{60}{80}, \frac{90}{120}, \frac{120}{160}, \frac{150}{200}, \frac{180}{240}, \frac{210}{280}, \frac{240}{320}, \frac{270}{360}$

3. $\frac{60}{80}, \frac{75}{100}$

Trail Mix Recipe (p. 18)
1. $\frac{12}{32}$ or $\frac{3}{8}$ **2.** $\frac{20}{32}$ or $\frac{5}{8}$
3. $\frac{25}{32}$ **4.** $\frac{22}{32}$ or $\frac{11}{16}$

Watermelon at the Picnic (p. 19)
1. $\frac{13}{24}$ **2.** $\frac{3}{24}$
3. $\frac{1}{24}$

Computer Repair (p. 19)
1. $1\frac{1}{12}$
2. $2\frac{2}{15}$
3. $1\frac{13}{20}$
4. $\frac{3}{4}$

Campground Rent (p. 20)
1. $\frac{52}{24}$
2. $\frac{30}{24}$
3. $\frac{73}{24}$
4. $\frac{32}{24}$

Hiking the Trails (p. 20)
1. 3 sandwiches
2. $2\frac{3}{4}$ km, $5\frac{1}{2}$ km
3. $2\frac{1}{2}$ hours
4. 1 hour. Answers will vary.

Class Report Chart (p. 21)
1. 0.6
2. 0.7
3. 0.3
4. 0.07

Ordering Tile (p. 21)
1. 0.08
2. 0.05
3. 0.42

Model Trains (p. 22)
1. 61.8 cm
2. 92.4 cm
3. 79 cm
4. 63.3 cm

Book Weights (p. 22)
1. 7.67 kg
2. 1.02 kg
3. 5.73 kg
4. 5.63 kg

Sharing Snacks (p. 23)
1. $\frac{1}{2}$
2. $\frac{1}{4}$
3. 0.6
4. 0.7
5. Either one. They are both equal to one half.

Votes for President (p. 23)
1. $\frac{1}{3}$
2. 0.75
3. $\frac{18}{20}$
4. 0.67

Daily High Temperatures (p. 24)
1. Tuesday
2. Wednesday and Friday
3. 30°
4. 42°

Student Body Election (p. 24)
1. Manuel
2. Denise
3. 80
4. 500
5. 125

Favorite Snacks (p. 25)
1. apples
2. ants on a log
3. 45
4. 30

Coordinates on a Map (p. 25)
1. a tree
2. a telephone/electric pole
3. a fence
4. a birdbath
5. in a park

Picking a Gem (p. 26)
1. 1:10
2. 4:10
3. 2:10
4. 3:10
5. 9:10

Picking an Outfit (p. 26)
1. 12 outfits
2. 1:12

Building a Birdhouse (p. 27)
1. 27 in.
2. 2 ft. 3 in.
3. 4 ft. board
4. 1 ft. 9 in.

Caterpillar Race (p. 27)
1. 18 cm
2. 12 cm
3. 45 cm
4. 15 cm
5. no

Wallpaper, Carpet, and Paint (p. 28)
1. 320 squares
2. 72 ft.
3. 24 yds.
4. 160 sq. ft.

Signs and Fences (p. 28)
1. 50 m
2. 154 sq. m or 154 m^2
3. 2 sq. m or 2 m^2
4. 6 m

Packaging Supplies (p. 29)
1. 1 cubic ft. or 1 ft.^{3}
2. 12 blocks
3. 8 blocks
4. C

Building a Raised Garden Bed (p. 29)
1. 306,000 cubic centimeters or cm^3
2. 1,000,000 cm^3
3. B. They would have topsoil left over.

$\frac{1}{2}$ cubic meter = 500,000 cubic cm, which is more than 306,000 cubic centimeters.
4. 1,285,350 cubic centimeters.
5. all in one trip

Sports Equipment (p. 30)
1. basketballs
2. 50 oz., $3\frac{1}{8}$ lbs.
3. a soccer team
4. 8 balls
5. 43 oz.; $2\frac{11}{16}$ lbs.; or 2 lbs., 11 oz.

An Elephant Diet (p. 30)
1. 112,000 g
2. 8 kg
3. 12,000 g
4. 132 kg

Taking the Ferry (p. 31)
1. 236,000 kg
2. 240,000 kg; 240 t
3. 440,000 kg; 440 t
4. no; yes
Challenge: 12.2 metric tons

Camping Schedule (p. 31)
1. 3 hours 20 minutes
2. 1 hour 30 minutes
3. 1 hour 20 minutes
4. 35 minutes
5. 25 minutes

Cycling for Charity (p. 32)
1. $\frac{1}{2}$ hour, 0.5 hr., or 30 minutes
2. $\frac{1}{6}$ of an hour or 10 minutes
3. $\frac{3}{4}$ of an hour or 45 minutes
4. 1 hour or 60 minutes

Canadian Time Zones (p. 32)
1. 9:00 A.M.
2. 7:00 P.M.
3. 5:00 P.M.
4. 8:00 A.M.

U.S. Money Facts (p.33)
1. 50 dimes
2. 200 nickels
3. 80 quarters
4. 500 pennies
5. Answers will vary, but coin values must total 50 cents, and three different coins must be included in each combination.

Canadian Money Facts (p. 33)
1. 20 dimes
2. 20 quarters
3. 20 nickels
4. Answers will vary. All combinations should equal $2.

Art Class (p. 34)
1. $14.01
2. $53.82
3. $16.25
4. $12.60
5. No, sold separately, the pencils and box would cost only $14.60.
6. $3.32

Yard Care Company (p. 34)
1. $4.05
2. $2.49
3. $1.30
4. $9.38
5. $11.45; $2.29

Trip Destinations (p. 35)
1. 23
2. 25
3. 16
4. 115
5. 841
Challenge: Answers will vary.

Favorite TV Shows (p. 35)
1. 860.4 or $860\frac{2}{5}$
2. *Mark Anders, Middle School Detective,* and *Talent Incorporated*
3. 316, *Dear Andrea*
4. 2007, Some are more popular than others. The results are not close.
5. 4,302
Challenge: Answers will vary, but could include that they would want to advertise on the more popular programs.

Carpentry (p. 36)
1. $\frac{5}{12}$
2. 3 pieces of board B, 6 pieces of board D, 4 pieces of board D plus 1 piece of board B, 1 piece of board A plus one piece of board B
3. 1 piece of board A, 2 pieces of board B, 3 pieces of board C, 4 pieces of board D, 1 piece of board B plus 2 pieces of board D
4. Answers will vary. 2 pieces of board B or 1 piece of board A

Pie Sale (p. 36)
1. $5\frac{2}{3}$ pies
2. $3\frac{1}{4}$ more apple pies
3. $8\frac{1}{4}$ pies
4. $3\frac{11}{12}$ peach and cherry pies

Perimeter and Area of Figures (p. 37)

1. $8\frac{1}{2}$ feet

2. $4\frac{3}{8}$ square feet

3. $1\frac{1}{4}$ feet

4. $\frac{1}{16}$ square feet

5. $4\frac{7}{16}$ square feet

Perimeter and Area of a Room (p. 37)

1. $49\frac{1}{2}$ ft.

2. $148\frac{5}{8}$ square feet

3. $34\frac{3}{8}$ square feet

4. $14\frac{1}{16}$ square feet

5. $197\frac{1}{16}$ square feet

Computer Time (p. 38)

1. 10 e-mails

2. $2\frac{1}{2}$ levels

3. $3\frac{3}{4}$ reviews

4. 5 friends

Art Projects (p. 38)

1. $8\frac{2}{3}$ squares

2. 13 squares

3. $14\frac{3}{4}$ squares

4. $11\frac{4}{5}$ squares

Keeping Track of Middle-Schoolers (p. 39)

1. 126 students, 14 students
2. 8 students   3. 34 students
4. 42 seventh-graders

Fundraising (p. 39)

1. $164.75   2. $12.77
3. $1,560.00   4. $1,416.00

Lemonade Fill-Up (p. 40)

1. 26 cups   2. 3.61 pitchers
3. 6.84 bottles   4. 18.57 glasses

Cancer Fundraiser (p. 40)

1. 25.25 bows   2. 6.16 gifts
3. 7.77 necklaces   4. 101 magnets

Basketball Percentages (p. 41)

1. 26%   2. 43%
3. 77%   4. 88%
5. Leo

Rose Garden (p. 41)

1. 25:50, 50:100, or 100:200
2. 10:15, 20:30, or 30:45
3. 50:10, 5:1, or 100:20
4. 15:25, 30:50, 60:100

Scale Models (p. 42)

1. 40 cm   2. 30 cm
3. 4 cm   4. 6 cm

Expanding Recipes (p. 42)

1. 7   2. 10
3. 20   4. 60

3-D Objects in a Flat World (p. 43)

1. a cone   2. a cube
3. a square pyramid 4. a sphere
5. a circle when lying down and a rectangle when standing
   The bases are circles, and the side is a rectangle.

Detecting 3-D Objects (p. 43)

1. a cube   2. a square pyramid
3. an octahedron   4. a triangular prism

Making Circles (p. 44)

1. 188.4 cm   2. 125.6 cm
3. 282.6 cm   4. 251.2 cm
5. 847.8 cm or 8.478 m

Ring Around the Horses (p. 44)

1. 157 m   2. 37.68 m
3. 157 cm or 1.57 m
Challenge: 3 m

Painting Triangles (p. 45)

1. 60 square feet   2. 96 square feet
3. 30 square feet   4. 160 square feet

Birdwatching Shelter (p. 45)

1. 72 square feet   2. 12 square feet
3. 18 square feet   4. 102 square feet

Insect Populations (p. 46)

1. 77 ants   2. 7 more flies
3. 21 more bees   4. 189 insects
5. 11:5 or 77:35   6. 4/5 = 28/35

School Desk Inventory (p. 46)

1. 60 paper clips   2. 150 tacks
3. 30 more pencils   4. 5:2 or 150:60
5. 300

Decoding a Message (p. 47)

2. The figure is an X.
Challenge: Answers will vary.

Soccer Spectators (p. 47)
Correct order as viewed from in front of the bench:
Brian, Tom, Jake, Becky, Carol
1. Becky   **2.** nobody
3. Carol and Brian   **4.** Tom
5. Jake

Temperature Changes (p. 48)
1. 25°   **2.** 17°
3. 20°   **4.** 9°C
5. 7 times hotter

Wrapping Boxes (p. 48)
1. Box 1: 2,256 square inches
      Box 2: 1,654 square inches
      Box 3: 4,198 square inches
      Box 4: 3,136 square inches
2. 11,244 square inches
3. surface area = (perimeter x height) + (2 x base)
      Exact formulas will vary.

Savings Account (p. 49)
1. $560   **2.** $22.40
3. $582.40   **4.** $1,164.80
5. $58.24

Class Can Collection (p. 49)
1. 400 cans   **2.** Class One
3. Class Two
4. Class One and Three   **5.** Class Three

Confused Equations (p. 50)
1. x   **2.** ÷
3. +   **4.** −
5. >   **6.** <
7. =

Carnival Prize (p. 50)
1. C   **2.** A = 42

Birthday Riddle (p. 51)
1. 32 years old   **2.** 16 years old
3. 9 years old   **4.** 12 years old

Reunion Leftovers (p. 51)
1. $\frac{1}{9}$ **2.** $\frac{1}{2}$

3. $\frac{1}{5}$ **4.** $\frac{2}{5}$

Fractions and Calculators (p. 52)
1. 0.417   **2.** the six kept repeating
3. $\frac{5}{12}$; Answers will vary.   **4.** Answers will vary.

Finding Prime Factors (p. 52)
1. a. 16   b. 2   c. 2
      d. 2   e. 2
2. 2 x 2 x 2 x 2 x 2 x 2 x 3